FIFTY WAYS TO A BETTER LIFE

Fifty Ways to A Better Life

ANDREW SERCOMBE

WORD PUBLISHING

WORD ENTERTAINMENT LTD
Milton Keynes, England

FIFTY WAYS TO A BETTER LIFE

Copyright © 1999, 2001 Andrew Sercombe

First published 1999 by Word Publishing,
a division of Word Entertainment Ltd,
9 Holdom Avenue, Bletchley, Milton Keynes, Bucks, MK1 1QR, UK.

British Library Cataloguing-in-Publication Data
A catalogue record is available from the British Library

ISBN 1 86024 345 2

Cover design by David Lund

Illustrations by Tim Charnick

Produced for Word Publishing by
Bookprint Creative Services, P.O. Box 827, BN21 3YJ, England.
Printed in Great Britain.

This book is dedicated to:
my wonderful family,
Sue, Elizabeth, Jonathan, and Ben,
Mum and Dad
and to
Campbell McAlpine

Contents

Preface

Although this is by nature an 'ideas' book, it is far from shallow. It has been written with the prime intention of offering you some life-transforming principles that really work. In a book like this the 'fifty' bit is a little arbitrary. You may see more than fifty, or only half a dozen ways to a better life. Either way, what I've put into these principles has been tried and tested over many years. I've really loved writing about them – so hopefully my own enthusiasm will be infectious too!

You'll read about real people in here – people I have worked with in my coaching practice. I've changed their identity a little for their protection but that's all. I hope their inclusion will narrow for you the gap that often lies between principle and practice.

Parts of the book can be particularly powerful if you are prepared to get deeper than just the words on the page. However, not all of them will work for everyone. The book doesn't pretend to be exhaustive or definitive, nor is it intended to be sophisticated. I wanted to write a book that is at the same time uncomplicated and interesting. See what you think.

One or two sections may, on occasions bring to the surface things that it may be worth the reader talking to a trained counsellor or personal coach about. Perhaps something doesn't quite fit: leave it for now and move to another chapter. You can always return to that chapter at another time for a further look. Who knows, it may be perfect for you later.

For the sake of variety I use different metaphors in different chapters and trust you not to mix them up! Another practical point is to have a pen with you as you read. I write in the margins of books I read and 'make them my own'. You may want to make some notes.

Of course, none of us is perfect quite yet, and that definitely includes me! Although these principles have been high on my agenda for many years, I still forget them sometimes or behave badly. I'm working on it though. I want to be the best I can be and the world to be a better place to live for the next generation.

I'm sure you do too.

Andrew Sercombe

Introduction

The principles this book contains, and the methods it uses, are guaranteed to change your life for the better if you take them seriously – when did you last buy a book with such a warranty! It is so rewarding to be able to see the changes happening when you thought you were stuck forever.

Even if you have been unable to afford the cover-price of this book and you're reading it surreptitiously in your local bookstore, or you've been lent it by a friend, it will make you richer. Simply turn the pages, select a chapter and read it with your mind wide open!

'Fifty Ways to a Better Life' is built upon the sure knowledge that your personal value has little to do with money, pension funds, personal capital and future earning capability. Its about the way you see yourself and your world – who you are, what you know, the experiences you have and how you use the resources in your personal 'bank' – that huge vault hidden deep inside the core of your life.

Surprisingly the actual money you have relates very little to the state of your personal bank. Becoming dependent on financial wealth or seeing it as a symbol of success, for instance, may even reduce the value of your core wealth. Other seemingly insignificant things, self-esteem, integrity etc., increase your riches out of all proportion. You'll see what I mean as we go along.

1. A Healthy Personal Ecology

Good foundations and a healthy personal 'ecology' are essential ingredients in a balanced lifestyle.

A pyramid and a lake . . .

Stable people have the pyramid of their life standing on its base, not on its point. Or like a lake with a healthy ecological balance, what flows out of your life is balanced by what comes in, so that you do not end up dry and barren. It means you will look at the quality of your lifestyle, ensuring that it is not polluted by input that will damage you. You will check to see that the boundaries of your life are well tended, that the richness of life within is contained and maintained, and that there is outflow as well as inflow. If you consistently refuse to share your life appropriately with others your 'lake' will slowly become stagnant and dead.

James was a little disappointed that Alfred had built the pyramid upside down. He spent a few moments wondering if it was worth telling him.

The Test

We all experience pressures and pain which test our theories and ideals – it's a fact of life! Trouble arrives at all our doors at some time or another, usually unexpectedly. It profoundly examines what we are built on, what we are made of and the state of the lake. It highlights weaknesses, develops and proves strengths. If you want to live positively recognise that pressure, stress and pain are part of your mature development as a person. You want a better life? Keep a lifetime of healthy balance, not primarily by juggling short-term bright ideas for instant relief (however helpful they are), but by building into your life immovable principles of truth that have been proven to stand the test of time and of history.

2. What You Sow Will Grow

You can't fool the system . . . well, not for long. So don't try.

The whole world runs on fundamental principles, laws of nature, that most of us are discovering all the time. A 'law' is something that always seems to happen. These principles are not just physical laws like the Law of Gravity, but principles that work in us as human beings and in our relationships. Laughter, for instance, is infectious. It spreads and grows.

Sowing and growing

A key law or principle to life is 'sowing and growing.'

Put potatoes into the soil, you get more potatoes out. Maize in, more maize out. No one expects to put potatoes in and get maize out! This applies to other areas of life too. If we live hating others, we will be hated . . . and inevitably hate ourselves. Those close to us, who imitate us, will start to hate people too.

You can sow what you like, where you like, when you like. Whatever you sow will eventually increase – often many times over.

Don't for a moment think you can violate this principle. You absolutely cannot. In the short term you can seem to get away with it, but eventually it will catch up with you. If I throw a ball upwards it seems to defy gravity, but it will eventually come down. Gravity insists on it. Look carefully at what you are sowing in your life. What do you want to grow there? How do you treat your friends, or your children? What you sow will grow. Do you save your money? Your savings will grow. Do you spend more than you have? Your debt will grow. Are you

You will reap what you sow. Don't think for a moment you can violate this principle.

15

hard-working? You will profit from your hard work. Are you lazy? You will have plenty of chance to be lazy in the future – jobless.

Add to this list other ways where this comes true:

- *Physical bodies:* The energy we put into keeping our bodies fit produces well tuned bodies that are able to do even more.
- *Children:* Rejected or abused children go on to reject or abuse others.

Don't think you can mess with these fundamental laws. Like the Taxman, they will always eventually have the last word.

It takes time

What you plant will not necessarily bear fruit straight away. It can take years. The longer it takes, the stronger the grip of the resulting outcome. Fruit that grows on the branches of an oak tree is directly related to what was planted, yet the fruit may not come to light for decades, and it may be a completely different generation that finally reaps the results of that

> A forest of oaks, or a back yard of toadstools? The difference is *time*

original acorn. However long it takes it will never change to a chestnut.

Ask yourself: 'What has been planted in me? What have I planted? What am I sowing now?' Be honest with yourself. Don't automatically accept the first answer you come up with! We are brilliant at fooling ourselves on the surface to make ourselves feel good. Living a better life involves an honest look at what can be developed and improved.

A generation apart

Let's look at an example. How you treat people will reflect the example you had in early life – how your parents treated people. Their worldview will have affected how you see things. You may have copied it or be madly fighting it. Either way, you are affected.

I was coaching a 39 year old man yesterday who held his head in his hands as he recalled the disparaging and demeaning way his mum had treated him as a child and teenager. He saw that, quite unwittingly, he was doing almost the same to his beautiful little children. His mum used to cut people dead if they didn't fulfil her 'reasonable' expectations of them. He had few friends – guess why? He had learned his mother's self-protecting skills, and raised huge castle walls around his life, only to find those walls had become his prison. He forgave his mum as we sat on the settee in his home, and ended the tyranny. He rooted out the growing seedlings and planted some new ones. He identified attitudes and a lifestyle that his girls could imitate and chose to live it for them to see. Thankfully he will be in time to see the new values grow in his kids lives as he feeds those values.

Food and famine

One way we can control what grows is through feeding it. If you feed a debt it grows. If you feed a cat, it grows. Our garden has looked really wishy-washy until recently when I applied some fertiliser. It made all the difference. It is now growing in abundance. The same applies to other things we grow. If you feed damaging things – revenge, hate, lying, meanness, gossip – they get worse. If you feed good things – compassion, generosity, being kind, courage – these will blossom and bear fruit.

Two sorts of growth: enlargement and multiplication

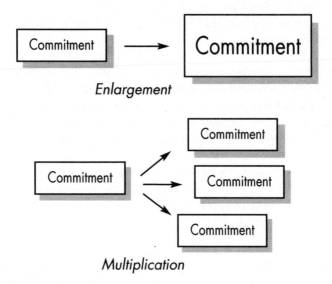

Enlargement

Multiplication

Embedded in the roots

This principle of sowing and growing is embedded in the roots of spiritual life around the world too, with most of the various religious cultures identifying a connection between the way you and I behave now and benefit in the next life. Hinduism and Buddhism have the concept of *karma*. Christians believe that our daily lives are being observed and recorded, and justice will be seen to be done in due course. Jesus Christ taught his disciples to 'lay up treasure in heaven' – an after-death investment resulting from discreet kindness and generosity here on earth.

3. The Not-So-Funny Farm

*A couple of years ago, not too far away from you, you may have
been able to visit a farm full of animals. They were all keen for the
farm to succeed so they had a meeting. The latest farming guru
was called in to let everyone know the best way for the farm to be
run to ensure it beat all competition.*

The farm was, in fact, already very good. They had top quality
animals, improving facilities and regular good weather. What they
did not have was all round competence, and this is what the guru
decided they needed. The animals were very good at their own
disciplines, but his concern was that the 'readiness to deal with
their weaknesses' was not there.

The PIGS' commitment to productivity was total. They gave
their all when it came to producing bacon, hams and pork, but
they were lousy at milk production. They sometimes 'borrowed'
milk from the cows to feed their piglets. The cows didn't mind.

The CHICKENS were producing the finest eggs in the market,
however they made the point that they needed to be sitting around
for hours in order to be successful at it. The guru complained
about their apparent inactivity. After some formal discipline
procedures, they were forbidden to sit around except at short pre-
arranged break times. Egg production suffered severely and the
chicken became very uncooperative.

The HORSES down at the stables had been groomed for many
years in body-building techniques. Their strengths lay in their
physical power and they knew it, and were proud of their
reputation. They worked hard for hours, with little let up and
would often compete with each other, playing games of 'chicken'
to spur each other on, but they became resentful at the guru's
suggestion that they should start laying eggs.

The COWS were the most inoffensive and gentle of all the farm
animals. They quietly got on with their task of giving milk twice a

day, quite uncomplainingly, doing their best to keep their attitude right when other animals told them to 'hurry up' or 'get a moo-ve on'. (Sorry!) When the older cows hurried, they hurt their udders. George the bull had stood up for them in a very protective manner. The guru eventually branded George a trouble-maker and sent him to market. No replacement was expected. Unsurprisingly, there hadn't been many calves or heifers joining the herd recently.

'Not-So-Funny Farm' closed a couple of months ago.

Let's state the obvious

Just as cows, pigs, horses and chicken have unique ways of functioning, so do human beings. The human brain is the most complex and intricate structure in the known universe, and yours is different from everyone else's. Foundational to a happy society is the discovery of each person's strengths and the freedom to go with them.

Identify the ways you function and relate to other people best.

(You may need to experiment to find out what your strengths really are.) Focus on what you are better at and promote it. Ask questions about how you as an individual – and people in your community – sometimes end up being destructive, selfish and bad, so that you can address those issues too.

Live as though your future depends on your positive choices. Make wise principle-centred decisions that benefit everyone, and be 'temperate' – don't expect everyone to have your abilities. You may also like to remember that our weaknesses are often our strengths taken just too far.

4. See Yourself Accurately

Someone once described humility as seeing yourself objectively, as you really are, to have a true perspective of yourself. Humility has nothing to do with grovelling, demeaning or devaluing yourself. Humility is not becoming the 'doormat of the world'. Humility is true self-acceptance, knowing what or who you are and what or who you are not.

'The biggest room in the world', my mentor and friend Campbell McAlpine reminds me, 'is the room for improvement'! We all have a place reserved for us there. Humility is accepting that there is room for change, that you can improve – and it is your responsibility to society to do so. It is also humility to recognise that some people are not going to change that much, and your trying to force them to will be damaging and counter-productive.

> **The biggest room in the world is the room for improvement – and we're all in it**

Idyllic perfection?

Blindly chasing after some idyllic perfection is a waste of time. Those who accept 'only the latest and best' miss out. Paradoxically, accepting only the best means you have very little. You miss out on the joys of the ordinary – which are often even better!

Most of us want to appear different from what we are inside. We create an image so that others will relate to us in a particular way. Of course that is part of normal life and our motives are mixed – pain and pleasure. However, the great danger is that I will create an image that I eventually believe to be real, and that may be very unhealthy. For some, wanting to be accepted is a more powerful motivation than accepting themselves as they really are.

It is impossible to live our lives without distorting, deleting or generalising the truth. Because of this we become adept at distorting truth in our favour. Not always a good idea!

You cannot always second-guess how others will see you. Your dentist and the window cleaner will see you very differently. Emotionally healthy people want to know themselves as they are and move on to develop themselves.

Bendable standards?

It is how you see you that matters, and whether your view is accurate. How are you going to decide on the accuracy of your self-perception? What standard will you use? What will be the 'good/bad' deciding factor? You need some unbendable standards to measure your life with. No builder or engineer would dream of measuring his work with a knocked up, home-made tape measure. He uses an established standard, a metre, or yard perhaps. So as you build your life in the future, what standard are you going to measure your life with? It is sickeningly easy to con yourself. And most of your friends will avoid being honest with you too! How will you know whether the foundations and walls of your values are true? Will you just quietly 'go with the culture' when deep inside you know the culture is distorted and harming your community and your children?

Standards you may use to measure yourself and gain approval

Everyone else
Religious beliefs
Parent's expectations
Company culture
TV images – soaps, homes, food, fashion, etc.
The blokes or women down the gym
The contents of lifestyle magazines
Stars of film, stage, politics, business
The people in your favourite magazine

Choose principles to live by that 1) have stood the test of time, 2) people have died for, and are, by their very nature, 3) absolute and unchanging.

5. Develop an Inclusive Mentality

Each of us affects other people. Your behaviour, attitudes and the things you say have an impact on those around you. Including those people, and keeping in mind how they are affected by you, improves *your* life as well as theirs. You become less selfish, more considerate and more like the people you admire the most.

People, or groups of people, who are affected by our decisions are called 'Stakeholders' in business. These two '*Oxford English Dictionary*' definitions describe a stakeholder. We focus on the second one:

1. *An independent party, with whom each of those who make a wager deposits the money, etc., wagered.*
2. *A person with an interest or concern in something, especially a business.*

Both of these imply that a contribution of some nature has been made, and the contributor is looking to gain something from his contribution – he sees it as a sort of investment.

When you include these people and groups in your plans and decisions you reduce any conflict between yourself and other people making life a whole lot more enjoyable.

Ask these questions:

- Who has had an investment in my life in the past? Do I owe them a debt . . . if so, what?
- What am I investing my life in right now? (Not just my money!)
- Am I investing in an ethical and productive way?
- Who is affected by my decisions?
- Who do I take into consideration when making decisions?
- To what extent do/should others' opinions affect the way I behave?

Do yourself and everyone else a favour: develop an inclusive mentality!

Jayne, a business consultant with Green Wright Messenger (GWM), a multinational accountancy firm, has been amicably divorced for two years. She has care of her two children (8 and 10) who have at last settled into a routine of seeing their father for an evening midweek and alternate Saturdays. This means a lot to the children, who love their dad, and to him – he misses them terribly. He has just been appointed to a local position in healthcare management on a five year contract. He turned down a very attractive promotion with his previous company because this new job will provide the children with the easy access to him they asked for.

Jayne finds it hard to make ends meet and GWM has offered her a substantial salary increase if she moves to an office 200 miles north. The new office is near her elderly parents who are becoming increasingly infirm and who she feels need her attention.

GWM, the company Jayne works for, has invested a lot in her training and will see a refusal to move as a lack of commitment.

Try this teaser for size. In this GWM scenario, imagine you are Jayne, and then the father of her two children. Choose a couple of these questions. Ask yourself:

- Who are the stakeholders?
- How does consideration and concern for each of them affect Jayne's decision?
- Jayne is a wise person. What decision do you think she will make, and why?
- How is her decision a reflection of your own priorities?

6. Let's Get Creative!

You have huge creative potential.

Following evening classes in computers, flower arranging and yoga, Monet decided to try just one more.

I don't enjoy hearing people say 'I'm not very creative.' It simply isn't true! We are all capable of creativity. We are doing it every day without noticing. Sadly most of us think of creativity in terms of art or decorating the bedroom. Maybe we'll think of creating our own family too. (I saw a fridge magnet yesterday that said 'Friends are the family you choose for yourself'.) All these are creative acts, of course, but creativity is vastly bigger than that.

Not every act of creation is constructive. Some people create horrendously destructive things. Our creative powers affect everyone around us and can bear wonderful – or downright evil – results.

> **Not every act of creation is constructive**

Creativity merely means bringing something into existence that didn't exist before. Here are some ideas of how it happens:

You can create . . .

- a productive or destructive atmosphere in the office or home
- sadness or joy in our parents or our children
- a smile or a frown on the face of a fellow passenger
- words that reassure and inspire a colleague
- a bank account
- a new hairstyle
- a violent argument
- a debt
- a window box of flowers or herbs
- a book, song, memo, love letter
- a memory

These are just a few ideas that I can rattle off on my keyboard as I sit here at the computer. You can create a list of loads more! Try it.

In fact it is impossible NOT to be creative. Simply by living we are creating things that didn't exist before. Every time we disseminate knowledge, sharing what we know, we are forming literally millions of electrical connections in other people's brains! I'm being creative in your head right now. (Scary isn't it?) I'm only interested in creating good, constructive, positive things in your life, so don't worry too much!

Constructive Knowledge Creation *increases* when:

- There is a thirst for discovery
- People experiment
- Every contribution is appreciated
- I discover something I didn't know before
- Another person discovers something they didn't know before
- I tell others what I know
- They tell others what they know
- We all learn from each other's mistakes
- I love my life

27

Constructive Knowledge Creation *decreases* when:

- I don't want to learn
- We stop experimenting
- Communication efficiency is reduced
- We hide mistakes
- I can't be bothered to explain
- Any contribution is devalued
- Relationships are damaged
- Knowledge is distorted

Here is a diagram to think about.

It shows how information is hidden away in our brains – information that we already know, but haven't realised we do!

Conscious

YKYK	**YKYDK**
Confidence	Enquiry
Most Use	Most Challenge
YDKYK	**YDKYDK**
Development	Humility
Most Encouragement	Most Fear/Excitement Unlimited

Knowledge

Subconscious

YKYK = You know that you know (Great!) This is knowledge that you are confident about and generally use. It is not complete, of course, in fact it will be distorted to some extent, but don't worry about that, most knowledge is.

28

YKYDK = You know that you don't know (Challenging!) I know I don't know much about golf. To date I've never really tried it, however I am beginning to get interested. I can feel my enquiry taste buds beginning to perk up. It would be an interesting challenge to learn to play golf. Am I going to learn?

YDKYK = You don't know that you know (Hidden!) Below the line of consciousness, in that hidden treasure house, are all sorts of things you don't know you know. Maybe you don't know you are an expert at reading body language. You are brilliant at it and do it all the time . . . unconsciously. You have practised it from birth. The workshops I do on Body Language help people to use the knowledge they already have by bringing it to the surface. It is very encouraging to find you know more than you thought you did!

YDKYDK = You don't know that you don't know (Serious!) This is the most worrying area on the graph, and the most extensive. Unlimited room for discovery. Steve Boyd is a friend of mine researching culture in some of the more remote parts of Thailand. When I visited him he showed me how I was offending the gentle southern Thai people without meaning to. Until he told me I didn't know that pointing my foot at them, or putting a hand on a person's shoulder is very rude. I'm quite a tactile person and know when touch is OK in my culture. However, the culture where he lives is mainly a 'no touch zone.' I love people and have no desire to offend. I didn't know I was being rude until Steve whispered to me to uncross my legs and put my feet flat on the floor, and that touching someone is regarded as very intimate and not done in public. Thankfully Steve's friends are very forgiving, so it was all right . . . just!

Get creative. Increase your knowledge. It will provide you with even more to contribute to the world.

Release the massive, hidden, unconscious resources you already have, and the unharnessed and unknown intellectual capital, creative insight, and emotional energies belonging to each and every person you know.

7. Keep Reading!

Clearly you are a connoisseur of books or you wouldn't be reading this one! Or perhaps someone gave it to you a few months ago and you have been struggling to get this far?

Books enable you to gain, as your own, the rich insights and wisdom of men and women from both the past and present. You can see the world differently by looking at it through their eyes.

Here are some simple principles on books and reading:

Leaders are readers

To influence the world for good you need to keep yourself fresh and have something life-giving to contribute each day. There is so much to learn from others – people who are specialists and you may never meet. Thankfully many of them have given us the privilege of knowing what they have learned for just a few pounds, dollars, or euros. They wrote a book – and you can read it!

Make the book your own

Make sure the time and money you spend on reading is worth it by writing notes in the margin and trying to catch the 'heart' of the author.

Avoid rubbish

Rubbish in, rubbish out. Life is too short for me to waste it filling up my mind with smutty, degrading, violent, or abusive literature. Whatever is honourable, whatever is of good reputation, whatever builds you up and is worthy of praise – fill your mind with these things.

Milk it of its value

A good book is worth reading more than once. Go back to it and re-read it. Then explain it to someone else. It is in explaining something to another person that we gain the greatest clarity in it. If what you read is good, put it into practice.

8. Discover Your Audience

Make a list of people who see the way you live.

They are affected by it and their attitudes affect you too. Scientists tell us that it is impossible to view something without changing it. Observing it changes it.

Note down a selection of people you come into contact with, at work, at home, socially, in your private life, etc. (Friends, enemies, clients/customers, colleagues, partner, children, parents, wider family, local community, bank manager, boss, people from the past/future, Inland Revenue, doctor, God, business friends . . . ? Write them down!)

If you could do so without being proud or showing off, what would you most like to show them about you personally? Write it down now. It may be something you've achieved perhaps or an aspect of your character.

Your Audience

Every good performer, from the concert pianist or comedian to the top football or basketball team player, knows how important the audience is to his or her performance.

Make friends with your audience. They are very influential. See those around as fellow students in the 'university of life', men and women, old and young, quick and slow, all of whom are living and learning. Listen to them carefully – they have a lot to teach you – but don't surrender control of your life to other people, or blame them. Your self-esteem will be harmed. YOU are responsible for you.

9. Embrace Your Responsibilities

The sort of life you lead, as a mature adult, is your responsibility. Because it starts with your own thoughts and inner life you cannot justifiably hold others responsible for what happens there for very long. Of course none of us is able to decide entirely what happens to us. We live in a world with six billion other people, and their attitudes and actions affect us, as ours affect them. As highly response-able people we decide how we are going to respond to what comes our way.

- Are you going to take on attitudes other people may have, and make them your own, when you haven't thought them through for yourself?
- Are you going to surrender control, fling open the door of your life to all and sundry and then blame them for what happens?

From then on, of course, you could justify or excuse your actions and wrong doings by saying it is their fault: 'I can't help what I think' or 'Everybody does it'.

To others and for others

You are responsible for your life and the affect of your lifestyle on others, whether you want to be or not. You are responsible both to others and for others.

The way you behave

You are responsible to the community in which you live for the way you behave. Each society outlines what it expects in its laws. If we do not want to be responsible to a particular community we must leave it and live somewhere else, in another town or country perhaps. Or we can decide to influence the community towards our way of thinking. People who refuse to abide by the expected standards of their society are generally isolated by it, either by being put in prison or shunned. However, sometimes they are right and society is wrong. History records the lives, and often untimely deaths, of many men and women who refused to accept the current values of the society in which they lived and went on to transform those values, making life better for those who lived around them.

A price to pay

Men and women who value human life and the freedoms of the weak and helpless above all, often accept imprisonment and rejection in order that others can go free. It is not by the way I treat the strong, the rich, the normal and the powerful that I will ultimately be judged. I will one day be held accountable for the way I protect, serve and support the weak, the old, the unborn, the crippled, the deprived, the disenfranchised. And none of us can use our politicians and leaders as scapegoats. In our western democracy they merely reflect the wishes of the people. You. Me. The truth is we pay a huge price now in lost 'personal peace'. Many men and women across the world suffer from a deep sense of purposelessness and worthlessness. You may do. Deep down most of us do not live up to our own standards of what we believe to be right or wrong, good or bad, let alone a higher or grander standard. We live beset by guaranteed failure, constantly trying to justify our motives and actions – to ourselves if no one else – in order to try and feel better.

'Rights' and wrongs

One of my personal principles is that human life is more valuable than anything else on earth is. It is of more value than other forms of life – animals, plants, etc. It seems to me that people have a spiritual dimension that other creatures do not have, and as a human being I react differently to

> Human life is the most valuable thing on earth

34

them. For instance, I am sad when I see a dead animal by the side of the road, but it does not affect me in anything like the same way as seeing an injured child by the side of the road. And size is not important either. I personally believe the smallest human life to be the size of a single microscopic living embryo.

I know that ethical issues are often not simply 'black and white'. There are many grey areas in life although I suspect there are actually fewer than it is sometimes convenient for me to admit to. However, the principles you and I need as a foundation on which we base our decisions should be clear and unbending. When you make decisions about human life based on convenience, economics and personal preference you devalue yourself and everyone else in the human race. With that devaluing comes the undermining of your own self-esteem, and your sense of personal worth and dignity.

The Universal Declaration of Human Rights?

I've spent a bit more time on this particular 'Way to a Better Life' because I'm convinced it is so very important. Its importance is highlighted by a poster on my study wall, a poster of the Universal Declaration of Human Rights.

These thirty Articles are so powerful! They illustrate how we are to treat one another as human beings. They remind us of each other's value. They seek to emphasise the dignity of humanity.

One Article we do not hear a lot about is Article 29 that reads:

'Everyone has duties to the community.'

Society will never be served satisfactorily by each of us focusing on our own rights – my 'right' to a particular quality and style of life and the attention and support I am 'owed' (each defined, of course by me.) That simply makes us more and more demanding and selfish.

Human rights and animal rights

It is interesting that those men and women in 1948 did not equate human rights to animal rights. We human beings have responsibilities that animals do not appear to have. Indeed, we have a profound responsibility to care for every aspect of our world, its wildlife and ecology, not least so that future generations can enjoy it too. When we are cruel or careless about creation we ourselves are the losers. Sometimes, of course, caring for it means leaving it well alone, protecting its anonymity. Margaret Wheatley in her brilliant book '*Leadership and the New Science*' reminds us that we cannot view, examine or monitor anything without interfering with it. That is a sobering thought. If you keep examining the roots of a plant, that plant is likely to die.

There will be no need to 'fight for rights' when we all focus on fulfilling our duties to the community and the world. Such a battle will have become irrelevant. We will all be too busy working to fulfil our own share of the communal workload to point the finger at where others inevitably fall short.

My Personal Mission Statement includes the line: *'To cherish the vision of a kind and forgiving world for future generations'*. I want to live with that vision well and truly cherished and work to make it happen. Perhaps you do too.

10. **Power Through Mentoring**

'Words, words, words. I'm sick of words. Show me.' Eliza Dolittle

Mentoring and coaching have become standard features of progressive businesses. Why? Because they work! Leaders have realised the benefits of making 'an experienced and trusted advisor' available to new staff, and have used the apprenticing model for training purposes.

Mentoring and coaching are similar but different. From my point of view, mentoring is about the way we think. It is about picking up attitude, not mere information, about the processing of life as a whole, as well as specific challenges within it. It deals with the deep motives that affect everything we do and are. Mentoring has been in existence for many centuries, and is about the journey more than the destination.

Thousands of men and women have found a significant increase in their own personal confidence and inner authority through having a wiser, older and more experienced person to whom they can refer and make themselves accountable. Example is an essential to effective mentoring. Parents, of course, are the most powerful mentors ever.

Coaching on the other hand is a little different. Coaching is more about the outcome of those deep mentoring roots – the destination. Whilst mentoring is more about where you are coming from deep within yourself, coaching is about where you are going to. Inevitably where you are coming from and where you are going to are irreversibly linked by the present. You are who you are now because of the past, and who you are now will affect, though not necessarily dictate, the future – and the outcome – of your life.

Role Models

What role models do you have?
Who do you most admire?

Why do you admire them?
Who would you most like to be like?

Ultimate Heroes

How valuable are 'ultimate heroes'?
Which are better: fantasy heroes or real historic ones?

Every day mentors

Mother, father, grandparents, an aunt or uncle, a favourite teacher, older brother or sister, explorer, sports or entertainment star, political figure, business personality, writer, etc.

Personal Mentor

Someone beyond yourself . . . in age, experience of life, (and possibly in experience of your particular task) who is 'walking in your direction,' etc.

Three meanings of 'Mentor' . . .

Hero / n. (pl. -oes)
1. a) Person noted or admired for courage, outstanding achievements, etc. (Newton, a hero of science). b) A great warrior.
2. The chief male character in a poem, play, story, etc. (*OED*)

Mentor / n.
An experienced and trusted adviser.
[French, via Latin from Greek Mentor, the name of the adviser of the young Telemachus in Homer's '*Odyssey*' and Fénelon's '*Télémaque*'] (*OED*)

Friend / n.
1. A person with whom one enjoys mutual affection and regard (usually exclusive of sexual or family bonds).
2. A sympathiser, helper, or patron . . . (*OED*)

Discover the power of mentoring. Get yourself a mentor who will develop your thinking. Seek out a coach who will show you how to reach beyond your perceived limits. Apprentice yourself to these people.

11. Get Accountable

One way to be accountable is to find a person who is wiser and stronger than you, who is trustworthy, and develop a friendship with them. I have a friend like that, with whom I am honest and to whom I open my life. He has a permanent invitation to say what he likes about the way I think and behave – and he does. His name is Campbell.

Campbell McAlpine, a wise and canny Scot, is my life mentor. For the last twenty-five years or so he has taken the trouble and time to help me, first as a young man, and now I am older, as an excellent friend and confidant. The benefit has been amazing. Campbell is an absolutely wonderful man, thirty-two years older than I am. He has been my spiritual 'Dad.' He is always encouraging, thoroughly honest, willing to give his opinion when asked, and is direct when I need it. When I was twenty-three years old I met him for the first time, and decided, immediately, that I wanted to get to know him better.

Our introduction went something like this . . .

'You don't know me. My name is Andrew Sercombe. I enjoyed your talk tonight and would like to spend some time with you.'

'Thaat's greet. How aboot six o'clock tomorrrrow morrrning?'

I dragged myself out of bed at five a.m. or so, and got to his house at six. He was waiting for me, and we spent two hours together that Monday morning . . . and every Monday morning that he was in the country for four years afterwards. He changed my life and, although he is eighty now, we still get together once a month or so. He still influences my thinking and behaviour and has unquestionably been the most significant influence in my life.

So what about you? You can be accountable to someone else! You can enjoy all the benefits of having someone mentor and advise you. Take your time to decide who that is going to be, and then go for it!

12. **Empty the Barn**

Elizabeth and I were walking along the sea front in Worthing. Elizabeth, my daughter in her twenties, and I were catching up on the latest in each other's lives. We enjoy one-on-one time whenever she comes home, and this was it, a brisk 45-minute walk with our active minds fully engaged and our mouths working overtime! We were talking about both of us being stretched and reaching our full potential, and about the way my business was developing.

Elizabeth quoted an old prophet who shouted to the people of his day *'Is there any seed left in the barn?'* This, she suggested, is the question I should ask of my life.

Over the following week or so I dug around in my 'barn' and saw that there was more that I could plant, that some of the seed had been hiding uselessly away in a corner and needed to be planted so it could grow.

Writing this book is a direct result of her question.

What seed is still in your barn? What resources do you have hanging around your life that could be of use to others? Make that seed, those resources, available. Sow them. What we possess is like manure, it is no good unless it is spread around. You may want to trade your resources or give them freely. Either way, ship them out where they'll be of use.

> Empty
> the barn
> – expect
> a harvest!

Empty the barn. Expect a harvest.

13. **Live Life in Colour**

The great President Roosevelt talked about *'. . . those poor souls who neither enjoy nor suffer much, because they live in the grey twilight that knows neither victory or defeat'.*

Avoid grey twilight like the plague! Break out of the ordinary! Live differently! Dare to go against the tide! Live life in colour! Our physical eyes lose their ability to enjoy colour as the light fades and shadows come. By living in the light we live life in colour.

I don't know 'where your life is at' as you read this. You do though. You know what parts of your life are being lived out in black, white and grey – or just grey. You know where fear has stopped you from breaking into a new job, a new career, or a new friendship.

In my work as a personal coach I have met all sorts of people who have suffered from the 'I can't' syndrome. They have looked at their lives and decided that nothing can be done. Wrong. Every person on this earth can live life in colour, for such living happens first of all in our thinking.

I used to go in to teach at our local High School from time to time. Regularly, I met teenagers who would say 'I can't' and I asked them whether they could if I gave them £1,000. Inevitably, the answer was yes, with a quick request to show them the money!

'Can't?' It's more about motivation than ability

The issue of course is rarely ability, it is usually motivation, and that is not ultimately someone else's responsibility – it is my choice. Am I going to live the rest of my life in grey twilight? Absolutely not! Am I going to surrender the life-giving sunlight of creativity to the dim shadows of mediocrity? Never! Will I allow the society in which I live to predict what I shall be? Over my dead body! Am I going to be

41

conformed or transformed? As you've probably gathered by now, for me that ain't a choice.

I don't care what it costs. I don't care if I lose popularity or short term respect. I don't care if it means a lower income to live on. I WILL NOT live out my life in the shadows. I will outrun the rat race and live differently.

Walking in the Light

Of course living life in colour has some other implications. It means that the hidden areas of my life may be revealed – not least to me. I may have quietly chosen to live in the twilight zone because I can hide there, or hide parts of my life that I would rather not admit to. Perhaps it is easier to just paint bright colours on the outside and use a carefully positioned floodlight to give the impression of living life in colour.

What a cramping, limiting way to be! How much better to be genuine, transparent. How much better to throw back the heavy curtains of hypocrisy, raise the blackouts of fear and let the sunlight flood in. It may be a shock to start with, but who cares!

What decisions will let more light into your life so you can enjoy living with richer colours? Start the process by making that first decision right now as you are sitting reading this.

14. Get Proactive in Making Choices

Managing your life

If you do not take control of your life, taking responsibility for what goes in and out and how your life is run, then other circumstances and people will do it for you.

Do you find a large spider or mouse running across the carpet – or even a sly work colleague – sometimes controls your behaviour?

When you feel in control of your immediate life, background stress is reduced. When you feel others are in control of your life, or 'circumstances beyond your control' arise, background stress is increased. When your immediate environment is unpredictable, or has substantial unpredictable factors within it, stress can increase dramatically. People are a major area for stress because they have a mind of their own and are not easily 'controlled'. What they do and say affects us. That is fine if we trust them to do us no harm, but experience tells us they often do! Allowing people we do not trust into our lives can cause havoc. On the other hand, trustworthy people are stress reducing. That is one reason why psychologists have found that a happy and secure family is such an important ingredient to a healthy lifestyle. We reduce stress by sharing our lives with those we love and who love us.

Masses of choices . . .

You DID NOT choose your parents, your first school, your height, your brothers and sisters, your blood group, your children, your genetic make up, or where you were born, but you can choose to make the most of every one of them, and loads more!

You DO have lots of choices every day. In our experience, even people who feel that they are the victims of their circumstances and feel imprisoned by them have choices that bring freedom and hope. Being in control of your life is very important. People who are controlled from outside, are rarely as happy, relaxed or physically healthy as those who are proactive in making decisions about their lives.

The process of choosing what I will or will not do and the person I will or will not be is called *SELF*-**CONTROL**.

Right now, identify three trivial and three important choices you can make:

E.g.

- What to have for breakfast
- Who my friends will be
- How to spend Sunday

15. Get Proactive by Avoiding Passivity

Fire burns, water drowns – and the day you make excuses instead of positive choices is the day the happiness curve on the graph of your life turns downwards.

When you are passive your clothes become shabby, your home deteriorates, your finances disappear and your children become undisciplined.

Physically
When a pianist stops practising his fingers lose their flexibility and his standard drops. If you lie in bed every day, your muscles waste away.

Mentally
People who think they 'know it all' and do not need to learn any more lose the skill of learning. To re-awaken the learning skill is a serious challenge.

Emotionally
Those of us who close down our emotions, soon find we are unable to feel anything significantly.

Spiritually
To surrender your will to 'fate', or anyone or anything else, finally results in you feeling unable to make a decision – often even a simple one.

Don't opt out. Opt in.

16. Me & Co.

As we have already seen, you are an interactive entity, relating to, and dealing with other people all around you. They will not work, live, or be friends with you for long if you expect a lot from them and provide nothing in return. Nor will you stay with them for long if you don't get something back from them. None of us likes one way friendship. In fact your life is remarkably like a business and looking at it as a business can be enlightening. Life is connections, and the connections are there for you to exchange with others.

You need to trade with others in life in order to live. We trade with time, attention, acceptance, friendship, skills, gratitude, wit, material and emotional security, approval, knowledge, care, etc. as well as with money. Whatever resources you have you can offer to others and receive something back. Bartering. Interestingly you do not always receive something back from the same person or at the same time. You may put something into your community, or into a club, and receive back 'communal' approval or acceptance. You may 'invest' in your children, giving them love and support, training for life, self-discipline, education, self-worth, etc., and receive gratitude and love in return many years later.

Building the assets of 'Me & Co.'

If you are going to be able to trade in the huge marketplace of life you have to have something to trade with. Those resources must be what other people want. (It is no good trying to trade with goods that no one wants. They don't buy them!)

Friendliness is an excellent product to develop. Enthusiasm is another. Both of these are appreciated and responded to. Others give us their friendship in return for our attention and care to them. An old proverb says 'He who would have friends must show himself friendly.' A trade!

You have 'customers' who will trade what they have for what they want themselves. Your perceived value in society will be dependent on what you can contribute. In fact your perceived value of yourself will be dependent on what you can contribute too.

Of course the worth of what we have to offer is different for different people and in different circumstances. Gold is worthless if you are starving to death. Food is what you need then. You may be able to exchange your gold for food, but you can't eat gold. If you have gold and cannot trade it you will die.

'Me & Co.' at school

That is why we go to school, college and university: to gain useful knowledge, and even more important, to learn the skill of how to gain it. If you are at school or in higher education – or any education – you will be able to see how you trade your time, intelligence, fees and attention for useful resources. You are responsible to develop your 'products,' what you have to offer, and that fits nicely with the concepts of 'Research & Development' in business. Appropriate knowledge is very valuable. If you have skills that are no longer required you must learn new ones. If you have been taught badly, perhaps by a mum who taught you to be selfish by her example, you must re-educate yourself, researching and developing new ways of behaving. Very few customers appreciate selfishness.

Marketing 'Me & Co.'

You are responsible for marketing yourself. How are you presenting yourself to others? How do they see you? – As hard and demanding? They are less likely to trade and you will probably end up alone and bitter – Fair and honest? You are well on the way to an excellent business!

Staying in credit

Like any bank account, taking out of life more than you are

willing to put into it will run you into debt. People will realise that they are not getting back as much as they are giving to you and will stop 'trading' with you. Again, if you dish out your resources to all and sundry and get nothing back from anywhere you will become depleted and unhappy.

'Me & Co.' at work

The principle of 'Me & Co.' also applies at work. Your boss may be your boss but he is also a customer of yours! When you give good service, keep up to date and work well, if he is a good customer he will pay well in expressed appreciation, good pay and more opportunities for you where they are available to him. If you do not provide what he wants, or he does not provide what you want in return for your resources, you will eventually find another job.

A good boss will know that you are a customer of his too. Unless he looks after you he will lose you to someone else.

'Me & Co.' applied to families

Sue and I are very different in the way we relate to the world and what we contribute into our marriage. We operate on fairly traditional lines in terms of our respective roles and it works a treat. We know what each other is good at and capitalise on using those strengths in each other. We 'trade' our strengths into our marriage and family and find them very complementary – thankfully! It has worked well for 28 years. However, both of us know how important it is to keep learning and stay flexible. What works now may not work tomorrow. We're always learning.

A family is a microcosm of the world and has lots of 'trades' going on. Brothers and sisters trade all the time; parents and children do too.

How? Think about it, or discuss this concept with a friend.

'Win/win/win'

A well known negotiating principle in business is 'win/win'. That means both parties in a transaction or deal get what they want in exchange for something they are prepared to release and the other person wants. I win in the deal, and the other person wins what they want too. I believe the best sort of deal is 'win/win/win'. That is when a third party, someone beyond both of us, wins when we do. 'Win/win/win' is amazingly powerful and raises us from a purely selfish business ethic.

How do you feel when you get 'lose/win' or 'win/lose' and you lose? How do you feel when your children or your parents win, and you lose?

See how many other people you can get to benefit from the trading you do in your life as you develop 'Me & Co.'

17. **Walk the Path to Freedom**

All the improvements we make to our lives start in our will. We talk about a strong-willed or weak-willed person. That will is all-important when it comes to dealing with passivity. Like any muscle, your will, or resolve, is strengthened by use. Strong-willed people get stronger-willed when they find their strength of will produces beneficial changes for them. Weak-willed people become weaker-willed when they find that their lack of resolve has made them even less able to decide.

'A ship in a harbour is safe, but that is not what ships were made for.'

Sadly, ships that spend too much time in a harbour rot and go bankrupt, with no funds to repair them. They are good for nothing.
   You are the master of your vessel, the driver of your car.
   Here are six 'orders' you can issue to yourself, as Master of your vessel, to get yourself out of harbour and towards your destination:

Order 1: Question your present Position

Change your mind about staying in this cosy harbour.

Order 2: Declare the Destination

Where are you heading?

Order 3: All Hands on Deck

No one owes you, and even if they do you cannot surrender your future (and the future of others in your life) to them. This trip will take your effort. Do EVERYTHING you can to achieve your goals.

Order 4: Take the Helm

Make a clear decision to go somewhere. You can't guide a static object.

Order 5: Cast Off and Set Sail

Even a small wire can prevent a ship heading to sea. You will never go anywhere if you are determined to 'be safe'. Considered risk is an essential part of life and is very important in our development. Of course, there is a lot of difference between risk and foolishness, but most people play too safe, well within their comfort zone.

Bon Voyage!

18. **Change is Here to Stay!**

'Nothing stays the same. The whole universe is altering and developing, and cannot reverse. Those who are best able to adapt to change are the ones who will stay emotionally healthy. Psychologists recognise that an ability to adjust to life is a very important sign of emotional health.' (Skinner, 1993)

Depending on your personality, change can be frightening or inviting. Some people love a change. Others prefer to stay in their 'rut'.

Both groups would provide logical reasons for their view . . . and why the other view isn't best!

Answering these five questions may help you see how enthusiastic about change you are.

Score '1' for Strongly Disagree and '4' for Strongly Agree.

Add up the total out of 20 and score it on the line below.

1. I really enjoy travelling – the further and more often the better!
2. I love a good discussion – especially when people feel strongly about things!
3. I like new things – whether they are clothes, a different car, job, or even house.
4. It is not important to have a reason to change. Fresh approaches always have their value.
5. People who always need to be right get on my nerves.

If you scored 5, you certainly prefer the status quo. If you scored 20, you are desperate for more change.

The importance of change

Change is another universal principle of life. Without getting too philosophical about it, there are very few things that don't change. By definition, truth doesn't change. The past doesn't change – although we can alter our perceptions of its influence on us.

> You cannot be the same person today that you were yesterday.

Most of the time we quite like change and don't notice it is happening. The children grow up, the seasons come and go – it would bring a great deal of sadness if they didn't.

Technological advances have meant that we have lots of opportunities we never had before. We can get out-of-date very quickly. In the past that would have taken a century or so. Now it takes only months. Change is accelerating, and many human beings are disturbed deep down as they try to adjust to circumstances a previous generation could never have imagined.

We have been thrown into a fast flowing river, and the current is increasing. To hold on to the riverbank will easily tear us apart.

How can we survive the trip? By understanding the river of change, learning how to use its opportunities, and adjusting. Trying to argue with the river does not work.

Changing your mind changes your LIFE

The ability to change what you think and the way you think is built in to every human being. Those who have acquired the insight to do this live more successfully, with more personal freedom and satisfaction.

Changing your mind can be as immediate and as permanent as switching a light on. It can happen in a second, and means that you will see things differently. The new viewpoint can never be taken away from you, although of course you are completely free to return to your previous view as quickly as you departed from it! Having discovered a new viewpoint, you now have two perspectives to see things from. You can add as many as you like, and change between them whenever you want.

Learning that there are new viewpoints, and seeing from them, is amazingly powerful.

How does change affect your family and friends?

When we change, or something powerful happens to us so we become different, our friends, colleagues and family are affected too.

Here are some major change scenarios which people like you and me face:

- Loss of 'permanent' work
- Winning the Lottery
- Death of a loved one
- Serious accident, injury or illness
- Big promotion
- Separation and divorce
- Moving house
- Financial loss (defrauded of life savings, etc)
- Having a first child
- Rejection by a close friend

These things may profoundly change us and, when we change, lots of other things change too.

What is 'good'?

To re-think and change your mind from doing something that is good to doing something that is better (or thinking something that is good, and thinking something that is better) does not mean that what you are changing from is necessarily harmful of itself; it's just not as good!

We define 'good' as fulfilling the intended purpose with ethical integrity.

What stops a person from changing their mind or seeing something from another person's perspective?

We change our minds very quickly in times of crisis or because of experiences that are often forced upon us by life. Quite suddenly, we see a person or a situation 'in a different light' and immediately change our opinion and attitude to them. We 'see' that our view was inaccurate, and update it in an instant.

Own it and change it

This week I was coaching a young woman with a child of five. Her son is autistic and often difficult to handle. His school struggles with him, and his mum, Clare, does too.

Clare was telling me how poor it was that the school refused to give her son the extra attention he needed. She felt that other mums should understand her little boy better and that the other children should be tolerant when her son hits them in the playground.

It was all everyone else's fault, and she was going to have another appointment with the head teacher to give her a piece of her mind.

I asked Clare how she thought the head teacher felt, having limited resources, and so many demands from parents like her. I invited her to imagine herself as the head teacher with Clare coming in to her office for a 'showdown.' As we considered the head's own frustrations and challenges Clare realised that blaming others was not the answer. She would feel like the other parents, if her own son was being knocked about by an unruly five-year-old. Blaming would not produce an answer. You can only change what you own, and she wanted change.

To her credit, Clare saw what she was doing and chose to change. Clare and I went on to talk about the effectiveness of her own life and the way she spent her time. Our lives, of course, comprise purely of time – perhaps 80 years or so. We have had half our life when we have lived for half that time, say, 40 years. What we do with our lives depends on how we spend our time, each day, each hour and each minute. How we choose to spend our time depends on our priorities, our passion, and our attitude.

Clare and I did a quick and fairly brutal assessment! Each week Clare has 168 hours to live. Ten hours per day given to sleeping and eating reduces this to 98 'programmable' hours. How did she spend this time? No fudging issues, or making jobs sound longer than they really were! Each activity was ruthlessly and honestly analysed for how much time it needed to be done properly.

However hard we tried we could only account for half that time. Clare had about fifty hours unaccounted for. That's 25,000 hours in ten years. 50% of her waking life was drifting away!

We discussed ways that Clare, who can manage financially at the moment, could use that time to be part of the answer, if only she were to stop allowing herself the dubious luxury of being part of the problem.

Her son loves books and can read remarkably well – even at the age of five. We discussed how visits to the library would motivate both of them. She said he would love that!

Clare could volunteer to provide the classroom assistance the school badly lacked.

Clare could research the particular needs of autistic children and become an authority on them, helping other parents, and understanding her own child so much better.

All of a sudden, it became clear that 50% of Clare's life need not be wasted at all. Her difficult child, and the hours she had were a God-given resource to motivate her and help other people at the same time as helping her own son. Her personal lack of discipline in the use of her time would give way to a much more responsible attitude. Her son could only gain from that improved example.

When you own it you can change it. Next time I saw her she had listed – to the minute – the way she had spent the last five days, and had implemented everything we had discussed.

Clare got richer, so did her son, and you and I have now benefited from her example.

Change – a personal story

Trauma

I will never forget the trauma of resigning from the church organisation I had served for fifteen years. I fulfilled all the negatives described on every psychometric test I've ever done. Pain, rejection, betrayal, disappointment – and a whole lot more indescribable reactions – swept over me, threatening to drown my shredded self-confidence forever. I had been working with this group of people as a full time job. I regarded them as my friends, and the way it all ended at the time became a source of the deepest sadness for my family and me. My decision to resign prevented further damage to me, to the family, and to the innocent majority in the organisation who had little or no idea of what was going on or why. They probably still don't.

So I resigned and started discovering a new world that seemed every bit as intimidating, challenging and seducing as that of any explorer. I felt quite strongly that I wanted to start a personal and corporate development consultancy. I wrote out a personal mission statement and eventually a business plan. It was a defining moment.

Brand new thinking

This was an entirely different way of life! The voluntary sector, of which most religious organisations are a part, is a world of its own. I had to learn, and adapt to this 'business world', a substantially new culture and a new language full of abbreviations, initials and business jargon I didn't understand. I had to change my lifestyle, my clothes, my car and even my watch! A lot of the time I was personally close to zero. Inside me pain and change were everywhere I looked. Yet I had to have answers and find where I fitted in. Inside I knew I actually did have those core answers, and would eventually gain the strength, courage, skill and insight to implement them.

The first priority was to gain knowledge and understanding of the culture in this new world. I needed it fast if I was to survive. I couldn't afford university so I decided to put into practice the principles I teach others and create my own 'university course' by reading the finest and the best of modern business writers. Dozens of volumes purchased, read, marked, learnt and inwardly digested meant I could feel myself changing. I went on every free course I could lay my hands on, and two that I had to pay for!

Slowly I managed to get some work. Redundancy workshops, communication skills workshops (I practised these on friends and family), supply teaching, one or two bits of simple 'consultancy', some personal coaching work, it slowly drifted in. I did various practical jobs to keep bread on the table, mending this and fixing that for people. (I remember putting a veranda on a huge chicken house containing 7,000 free-range chickens. They were inside; I was out in the cold and rain! I was very grateful for the work and the money.) Always there was a business development book close at hand. I knew I would eventually have the inner resources and saleable knowledge I craved.

First hand

However, what I needed most was a new sense of self-belief – to know and be confident again in who I was inside – as this part of me had experienced serious damage. Below the surface I was maximising the first hand experiences I would need for the future. I was not merely learning about running a business, handling major change, the new order in the global corporate world, or about 'lifetime learning', but actually experiencing what they feel like, why they are important and how best to embrace them.

There are a lot of great people in the world! Some helped because they loved us a lot and were simply genuine friends. I am sure some people helped me out of pity. Whatever! I was particularly grateful for those high up in the business world who believed in my vision, mentoring and educating me. Paul in particular was brilliant (in several senses of that word!) He and I have spent many happy hours in both gym and sauna thrashing out various issues (verbally, that is), and we continue to do so!

Light at the end of the tunnel?

Today my business, 'Powerchange' continues to develop. What I know is proving useful to others' prosperity. (I've even had a client tell me I was underselling myself and give me a cheque for double what I charged him!) People phone me as well as me phoning them. I no longer have the crippling desperation in my voice. We have managed to keep the house and stay free of major debt. And I'm fulfilling what I know is my life's purpose – and getting paid for it!

19. **Dream On . . . Please!**

'Fear not those who dream by night. Fear those who dream by day.'

I don't know who said those words but he or she was dead right! Everything mankind has ever made or done started as a dream, a thought, an inspiration. The chair you sit on, the computer you use, the clothes each of us wears, the cars we drive, the books we read . . . everything started as an invisible idea, so please, please keep dreaming!

Dreaming really will change your life and your future.

Dream about what you can be. Dream about how you can change the world – and you can. Dream on. As you think in your heart, so you are. Change what you think, by imagining yourself and your world beyond today, and tomorrow will be different. Let your mind conjure up new ideas, new thoughts. Invite your imagination to go to work on the challenges you face, and you will be amazed how many of those challenges it will produce solutions to or shed light upon.

We were designed to dream. Fulfil your destiny.

Some people are afraid to dream. They are concerned that it will put them into 'cloud cuckoo land' and they will become dissatisfied, or frustrated. Or they are afraid their dreaming will

> **We were designed to dream**

bring sadness as they consider the longings they had in times past that were disappointed. Perhaps you are like that right now: 'I dreamed and it didn't work out.'

I would like to suggest it was not that you dreamed too much, but that you dreamed too little. When one dream was unfulfilled you refused to dream some more, or just didn't bother.

Of course not every dream comes true. No one would want that!

Some dreams are damaging to ourselves or to those around us, so we are better off without their fulfilment. However the answer is to keep dreaming, to produce more resources from within the creativity of our minds. Many of these dreams come true as we pour our creative energies into and over them. We slowly but surely see the evidence before our eyes.

Some people need to see before they will believe. Others have the ability to believe before they see. Dreaming is the raw material of the physical reality. Without the dream there will be no evidence.

Are you going to leave the dreaming to others or are you going to have some fun yourself?

Dream on . . . please! The world needs you.

20. Develop Healthy Defences

I remember well someone saying to me, in a critical, superior and aggressive sort of way, 'Don't get so defensive!' I wanted to reply bluntly, 'Then stop attacking me'.

Whether they were actually attacking me or not is beside the point. I thought they were, and that is why I reacted as I did (probably without realising it.)

You may get defensive when you subconsciously feel vulnerable and untrusting towards a perceived potential threat. That may be an important exam or a threatening conversation or interview. Perhaps the other person has a reputation for being judgmental and you don't trust his judgement. Or maybe she gossips and you have no desire to be fodder for her conversations. Perhaps they have a loud overbearing style, or you just feel thoroughly inadequate in their company.

Whatever your reason, however justified your reservations, it is important to have defences that do just that – defend. Ask yourself: 'What would it be like if I didn't get defensive?'

Defence, not attack

Contrary to popular belief, the best form of defence, generally speaking, is NOT attack. Attack brings alienation, even more aggression, and breeds long-term enemies. Healthy defensive systems reduce aggression, diffuse tensions, and limit damage. They can easily be developed, and are immensely useful. They *de*fend without *off*ending.

Wall building

One way you may have defended yourself is by building walls. Normally these are high, too high to see over. As life goes on, the walls become more and more numerous as more people are excluded, cut off from effective communication with you. You may eventually become surrounded by these big and little walls. They become your 'prison'.

These walls can become permanent, the concrete setting over the years until the barriers you erected have trapped you. You live your life weaving in and out of these walls, using up your energy 'wall dodging' or simply unable to go anywhere.

Temporary walls are OK for a bit. They enable you to heal and gather yourself. Never make them permanent though. Take them down at the earliest opportunity.

Temporary walls are OK for a bit, but soon they'll trap you

Effective self-defence

If you want a better life learn to defend yourself effectively, remembering the following points:

1. It may be possible to diffuse any thought of attack both in your mind and theirs.
2. Keep conversations moving. Don't get locked in to minor opinions – yours or theirs.
3. Listen to yourself in the conversation. Perhaps the other person has decided their best form of defence from you is to attack, because you come over more strongly than they can handle comfortably.

Here are four practical strategies for you to consider:

Look ahead

Ask yourself what might come up when you talk with this person. Prepare a mature response to it that damages neither of you and practice saying it if necessary. Make sure the tone of your voice and the way you sit or stand is unthreatening. (Or revise properly for the exam!)

Undress it!

Most threatening situations are more to do with how we see them than how they really are. Have you ever imagined a policeman standing in his underwear booking someone, or a senior executive in their pyjamas reprimanding a member of staff? What a thought! When we mentally strip people of their dark uniform or smart business suit they symbolically lose their power. (What do you think uniforms are for?) 'Is anyone over-reacting round here?'

By the way, for all those at school or University, the 'intimidating' examination environment is only provided so that you can give your best without anyone gaining unfairly. Use the peace and quiet of the exam room to your advantage.

Detox it

Take the venom out of circulation. Let the person have their say, get it all out, go mad at you, etc., and although you feel the pain, choose not to spit back. Store up your frustration and anger so you can vent it at another time and place – somewhere safe where its expression can do no damage. (NOT necessarily your partner or the cat!)

One really helpful way to detox is to write a letter to the person telling them exactly what you think – loud, long and hard – then tear it up instead of posting it. It is safer in the bin. You may need to be honest with them about their behaviour and its affect on you at some other time and place when things are less tense. Or you could work out the pain in another aspect of your life, by going for a long walk or run, a hard game of squash, or beat up a cushion! These days there are effective ways of getting emotional pain to disappear completely. We use them in our coaching. Controlling your defensive reactions until you are in a safe place to express them has been shown to actually increase inner strength.

Stand back

Not literally of course, but in six months time, or even after a good night's sleep, this situation may not seem quite so important. See the lighter side, see why the person is actually responding this way, and do all you can to validate their view. Agree with the things they say wherever you honestly can. They are saying these things for what, to them, are very good reasons. Find out what those reasons are. 'Standing back' also can mean asking for time to consider what they are saying before you respond.

Graciously give them the space to change their minds without them having to apologise. Next time you meet they may be wishing they hadn't been so 'over the top'.

Give people space to change their minds

21. **Understand Fear**

Fear is the physical feeling and emotional response to 'fears' – those real, imagined, or anticipated circumstances in our lives that we find very unpleasant for all sorts of reasons.

Fears are usually learnt very quickly and are typically the result of a single learning experience. The feeling of fear shows that your brain can learn very quickly!

Fear is a communication from your unconscious mind. It is attempting to communicate to you that perceived danger is present and that you need to be very careful. 'Irrational' fear is due to your unconscious mind linking, or associating, strong negative feelings from the past to present situations and imagined future expectations. It often cross-links to the fears of others: 'He/she is afraid so I need to be.'

> **The question is: Is this fear controlling me?**

Your mind does not always accurately differentiate between reality and imagination. Research shows that not everything we remember has actually happened! Witnesses in Court will sometimes deny under oath that they said something even when they have the videotapes played of them saying it – and they mean it. Our memories really do play tricks on us!

We sometimes use different words to express the fear we are feeling – apprehension, worry, anxiety, concern, etc.

We can react in different ways. Fear has as its root the desire to run away. The Greek work is Phobos – we use the word 'phobia' – and it means 'flight.' To fight what we believe to be the source of our fear is another option.

Fear and stress are both closely linked to being out of control, or being in the control of another dominating person or situation.

Why have we been given the ability to feel fear?

- Fear stops me becoming complacent
- Fear stops me doing wrong
- Fear keeps me close to my deepest convictions
- Fear reminds me that I'm not super-human
- Fear produces the adrenaline I need to get me out of danger
- Fear stops me being impetuous
- Fear brings (healthy and unhealthy) respect
- Fear makes me fight
- Fear makes me run away
- Fear develops endurance and character (we decide what!)
- Fear motivates me to change things

When is fear unhelpful?

- When it dictates our lifestyle and health
- When it becomes injurious to us or others

'Out of control' fear produces:

- the experience of panic, terror, etc
- physical injury within our bodies
- violent, often unpredictable, reactions

Ask yourself: 'What could I have instead of controlling fears?' Both fear and excitement produce similar physiological responses. The main difference is the expected outcome. 'What would happen if I decided to use the word "excitement" instead of the word "fear"?'

22. Keep Your Eyes on the Prize

Maybe you haven't got a 'prize' to go for at the moment. Now is the time to decide on one.

Obsessive goal chasing is not entirely healthy of course. Men and women who have become over zealous about their goals tend to destroy everything else – and sometimes every one else – around them. I don't want my family to suffer because I am obsessively chasing goals. Many a son has grown up longing to have known his father and many a partner suffered loneliness and rejection because her other half was never there, so I want to be a good dad and husband. Remember, the journey is as important as the destination and the way we live is as important as what we live for.

Yet most of us do need something to go for. Aim at nothing and you'll hit it every time! And the most important things to go for in life are invisible, intangible. They don't respond to spirit levels, calculators or tape measures. They are usually spiritual values and goals.

> Most of us
> DO need
> something
> to go for

One of my personal goals

Like a significant majority of people in Britain, according to a recent survey, I believe in life after life. I believe in a God who often interacts with us here and now and I can't wait to be in heaven with Him forever when I die. Death for me is a gateway to somewhere much better than here. So the ultimate 'prize' I've got my eyes on is God's approval of the way I have lived on this earth and what I have achieved with my time and talents. I am aware of God watching me – because he really wants to reward me – and that awareness certainly affects the things I do and think. I want him to be delighted . . . really pleased! I want to hear Him say 'Well done, Andrew!' That is my stated 'prize'. It has nothing to do with a big pension fund (it's just as well!) or world recognition – though both of those might be attractive in their own way. I want a prize that lasts forever.

What do you want?

23. Choose to Enthuse!

Question: *Name the one thing that's more contagious than enthusiasm.*

Answer: *Lack of it.*

Attitude, Attitude, Attitude

Attitude is everything in moving forward. Negativity, however understandable and justifiable, doesn't work and is known to damage us as people. We have to deal with it.

How?

If I were to pay you £5,000 in exchange for five ways to deal with negativity – in the next three minutes – what would you come up with?

It isn't always easy to keep that positive attitude, but negativity uses up huge resources of emotional energy.

You need all your energy to find positive solutions to life's challenges.

Here are some ways to help that:

- **Watch your language.** Critical and judgmental talk blocks the flow of positive energy. Make sure you speak positively.
- **Watch the company you keep.** Stay away from negative people when you can. Spend time with wholesome encouraging people.
- **Watch your fuel gauge.** What goes in is what comes out. Foul and abusive talk in, foul and abusive talk out. See that the input into your life is helpful. Don't get caught with TV programmes or magazines that sap your enthusiasm or fill your mind with rubbish.

- **Take 30 seconds.** Every now and then be quiet for 30 seconds or so. Take mental stock – renew your perspective.
- **Time with choice friends.** Choose your close friends very carefully. True friendship is about wanting the very best for that person. Check it out – do your friends really want the best for you?

Passion

Passion is a misunderstood concept. It now has predominately sexual implications – bodies intertwined in the latest TV series – or screaming at a football match. Mention passion and kids giggle behind their hands. Sadly, unless you are being passionate about a narrow band of culturally acceptable issues, too much enthusiasm is frowned on. You're regarded as an 'anorak' or 'train-spotter', a sad case without a real life.

True passion, of course, is so much more full than these limited perspectives. It is the energy that gets people up and going, the food of the creative genius, Olympic athlete and motivating entrepreneur.

Choose to enthuse

Whatever you do, do it passionately! Live with enthusiasm bubbling from within! If something is worth doing, do it with courage, boldness, conviction; and more than that – encourage others to be passionate in what they want to do. Enthuse over their interests. You have a friend who likes jam making? Choose to enthuse. Stamp collecting? Choose to enthuse. A new non-prestigious job? Choose to enthuse.

Why pour cold water over a newly acquired interest just because it doesn't fit your own narrow prejudices? Too many do that. Choose to enthuse.

> Only one thing is more contagious than enthusiasm: LACK OF IT

I read recently that in the first 18 years of your life you will have 15,000 positive affirmations, mostly in the first three years, and 225,000 negative ones. Is it any wonder we live cramped limited lives? I've looked at my own attitudes over recent years and seen too much criticism of others, too much judgement. I don't want to throw away my brain and enthuse over everything, regardless of its value to society, but to be honest, most things people take an interest in are hardly life-threatening or damaging. If they could do with someone to add energy to their interests, I'll do it! I'll choose to enthuse.

Campbell has a favourite prayer: *'Lord, save me from being gullible and suspicious!'* Having echoed that little prayer myself, I've set about being part of the answer to our dispassionate society. I believe in what I'm doing, and will do it with passion, conviction and enthusiasm.

You want a better life? Live it with true passion.

24. Be Part of the Answer, Not Part of the Problem

You have so many opportunities to praise and support others. Deciding to be cheerful, smiling (not manic grins, please!) and making 'contact' lifts people's spirits, gives them a better day, and is a rewarding way to live. So many people have lived horrible lives, and come to work to escape from the stresses of home.

A salesman (a good one too!) came for a consultation recently. He was afraid of his two late-teens, martial arts-trained sons. If they didn't get their way they would threaten their father and smash up the home. A gentle man, he was very intimidated and had lost so much – including the respect of his family – and despised himself.

Another client, a twenty-year-old girl, attractive, vivacious, bright, tagged herself onto the end of a consultancy list I was doing for a company. She told me her story. Her mum was a prostitute and had started to introduce her daughter to her customers at the age of twelve. At fifteen she was taken into local authority care. A handful of schools and jobs later she was living behind a cast iron mask. Able to smile and technically do her work, she was unable to bring anything of herself to it for fear the mask might slip. She readily admitted to manipulating people. Huge chunks of her personality had closed down in order to reduce the risk of severe emotional pain.

For both these people – and millions like them – personal confidence, self-esteem and a sense of dignity had gone out of the window years ago, leaving behind a legacy of caution, negativity and suspicion.

Mend it!

Thankfully so many of these situations are repairable, and you can help repair them! If you want to live a better life then be part of the answer not part of the problem. Boost people's self-esteem. Value them as human beings even though you may not naturally like them very much. Curb your criticism. Stand up for them – even when you don't agree with what they say or do. We can separate the people themselves from their present opinions and behaviour. They might have changed their views by next week and their behaviour by next month! There is no such thing as winning an argument, so be gentle if you must disagree. It is so easy to win an argument and damage a friendship. Better to bite your tongue. Who says you are right anyway?

'Professional' care?

And while we are on the subject, you don't have to be a professional to care for and help others. It is very easy to use the excuse of our lack of skill to avoid getting involved with the struggles others have to face. 'I'm not a Social Worker.' 'This isn't a charity.' 'I'm not a psychiatrist.' Of course some things are best left to those

> Remember: amateurs built the Ark and professionals built the Titanic!

who have studied mental illness, or whatever it happens to be, but all of us can care. There is enormous pleasure in giving something of ourselves. I've discovered so much by listening. Some of my most formative moments have been when I chose to sit quietly and empathise with another human being. Many need no more than some time and attention. They need a person not a quick fix. You and I can be that person.

25. Live Your Beliefs and Values

Take a look at these two tower illustrations

Tower 1

Are there areas of your life that are out of tune with your deepest convictions and beliefs?

Look at ways of bringing them into line with what you know to be right, just and true.

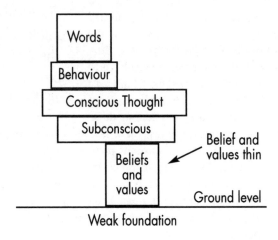

Weak foundation

Tower 2

In this tower, words and beliefs line up with beliefs and values. This is more like it!

This person has a lot more credibility and integrity. Thought out beliefs and values, behaviour demonstrating the validity of what is both said and thought. I would trust a person like this. This is how I want to be.

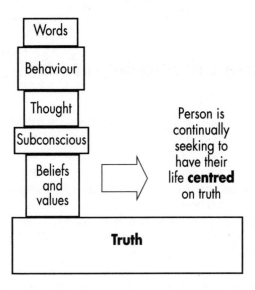

'... to tirelessly work to narrow the gap between principle and practice, whilst making fun, passion and care part of our daily lives.' Body Shop International

26. Audit the Bank Account

As we have seen, every individual has a selection of beliefs, values and principles that govern the decisions we make and the priorities we have. These are often quite subconscious, being instilled into us by our upbringing and by traumatic or significant events or relationships we have experienced. Many people don't recognise them. These things govern 99% of what we do and say, how we see our world and how we respond to it. But not all these beliefs, values and principles are healthy or best for us and for those we love. When these beliefs, values and principles come to the surface it is quite easy to recognise the good ones, and a bit humbling to accept there may be unhelpful ones. Most of us would agree that beliefs, values and principles that are harmful to us are best got rid of – when we eventually identify them of course!

Consider this statement (you may like to discuss it with a group of three or four friends):

'The greatest single cause of damage to people, including ourselves, is to live, or be forced to live, in a way that goes against our deepest understanding of what we believe to be right and just. It is an integrity issue.'

Brighton Rock

A life of integrity is like a stick of Brighton rock. It says the same thing wherever it is cut!

What is it that governs your decisions?

Choose 'Six of the Best' from the list below, or identify others that are not included in the list that fit you even better.

Some Beliefs, Values, Principles:

POWER, SELF CONTROL, DIGNITY, FREEDOM, ORDER, HAPPINESS, HARMONY, FAMILIES, TRUTH, HONESTY, BEING WEALTHY, PLAYFULNESS, REVOLUTION, WORKING WITH OTHERS, MAKING THE WORLD A BETTER PLACE, HAVING A RELIGIOUS FAITH, MAKING THE MOST OF YOURSELF, BEING ELEGANT AND FASHIONABLE, EXCITEMENT, MASTERY, LOVE, HOPE, CREATIVITY, LEARNING, SPORT, THE LATEST TECHNOLOGY, YOURSELF, T.V., YOUR PARTNER, YOUR CHILDREN, FOOD, EDUCATION, STATUS, RESPECT, FRIENDSHIPS, REVENGE, PERSONAL PLEASURE, SEX, PRINCIPLES. WORK. MONEY. HEALTH.

27. Clean Up

Take a moment to imagine yourself quietly wandering through the vaults of your own personal bank, the bank of your life, deep underground.

- Look around and identify anything that is devaluing you or not worthy of you. Look through one area at a time: childhood memories of things that people said to you and about you when you were young; the way you behave or are treated at home or at work; your conscience; anything you have to try and justify; the attitudes you take – perhaps to one person or another.
- When you become aware of each devaluing thing, shrink it to the size of a thimble and crush it under your heel. Why should you tolerate anything in you that lowers your self-respect, cuts down your confidence or is a secret embarrassment? You can take the authority you have and order it out! Get rid of it by imagining yourself removing it to the exit of your bank. Load it onto a refuse truck and watch the truck take it away forever.
- You can exchange an unworthy or devaluing item for something better. Replace a poor attitude towards a colleague with a really good one. Replace a dominating bad memory of childhood with one you treasure.
- It may be possible to repair an item that is broken – an old friendship for instance. (There is help elsewhere in this book on just how to do that.)

Remember, you only want good things – assets in the bank of your life. Bad things have a habit of affecting everything near them. Be careful not to compromise.

28. **Personal Freedom**

Hold half a matchstick (or some other similar item) clenched in your hand, as if someone wants to get it and you certainly don't want him or her to! Imagine that holding on to that half-matchstick is very important to you.

Now try to do a whole lot of 'normal' things, or imagine yourself doing them, without letting go of the half-matchstick. Combing your hair, having a bath, driving the car, getting dressed and eating a meal, hugging a child or friend. Remember, you must hold tightly onto the matchstick.

1. How does your grip on the half-matchstick affect these things?
2. If the item you were holding on to were something of immense value, a jewel for instance, you wouldn't want to discard it. What would you do with it?
3. If what you hold onto is damaging or unhelpful to you or those important to you, what would be best to do with it?

Take a look at what that gripping has done to your hand. It has become a fist.

Memories can be like that half-matchstick. Many people, of all ages, live crippled lives because they have chosen to hold tightly onto something from the past: a past hurt, grievance, or offence – or find they are locked in to a relationship or job that has gone. Gripping on too tightly, even to good things, can destroy your freedom. So how can you live with personal freedom? How can you be free of life's half-matchsticks?

Free from the limitations of Good Things

Holding on too tightly to good things isn't a good idea!

Stephen, 55, lost his wife eight years ago. He decided he couldn't move to be nearer his children because it would be disrespectful to the memory of his wife to move away from the village where she had lived (although deep inside he wanted to).

Phoebe refused to learn the latest accountancy software. She held that she had won a national award in 1983 without it, and was unwilling to accept that times had changed. Eventually she had to leave the company.

If this is you today I suggest you follow this procedure – or create a releasing one of your own:

1. Find a symbol to represent each past situation. A pebble, a photograph, a sheet of paper on which you have carefully described the situation, or it may even be the half-matchstick!
2. Take that symbol and find a very safe place for it. You may want to bury it somewhere, literally put it in a safe deposit box, perhaps lovingly cremate it or drop it into a deep river.
3. Mark the spot so that you can return whenever you like and enjoy the happy memories to the full.

Free from the limitations of Bad Things

Thirty-seven-year-old Caroline had become very bitter. 'Men are all the same. My dad was very violent to my mum and me. I will never trust a man again. You never know what might happen.' She had few real friends and lived as though she didn't care. Only Caroline knew just how lonely she was.

If there was one person who was the life and soul of any party it was Carlos! He filled his life full to the brim with socialising and effervescent activity. He had to. Seven years previously he had been cheated out of a great deal of money by a business partner, and had coldly decided never to forgive him. The resentment had fermented away. Carlos was now being treated for a serious stomach ulcer that the doctor had suggested may be linked to stress. Carlos knew it was.

Stephen and Phoebe were holding on to good things and needed to let go in order to live freely again. It is important that they can 'access' those happy memories when they need to, of a loving wife, and a national accountancy award.

Caroline and Carlos are holding on to things that will actually destroy them inside. They have nothing of value to lose, and everything to gain – not least health and happiness. The faster they get rid of their half-matchstick the better and they will immediately start feeling better.

Here is the process for Caroline and Carlos:

1. Find a quiet place where this process can be completed quietly, significantly and uninterrupted. You may like to share it with a trusted friend as a witness.
2. Look at the clenched fist containing the problem half-matchstick. Open your fingers, and carefully invest in that little centimetre or so of wood in the palm of your hand all the resentment, hatred, bitterness, etc., that you feel, and along with it the wrongs themselves.

'Caroline, put all the dreadful memories of your Dad's disgraceful behaviour into that matchstick.'

'Carlos, first of all you need to invest into that matchstick the foolish decision you made never to forgive. In making that cold revengeful decision you created a wall across the pathway of your life. That decision has actually been far more damaging than the lost money. Only then can you put into that little piece of wood the original wrong. (Do that too of course!)'

3. Think of a satisfying way to destroy that matchstick, and all the damaging memories it contains, completely and forever. Be creative . . . dream up three or four different ones and choose a particularly good one from those. Obviously, it needs to be done in a safe way for you and everyone around you.
4. Do it now. Get rid of every vestige of that matchstick and its contents, and go and enjoy your personal freedom from those things.

29. Conciliation Ecology

Conciliation Ecology is about creating an environment, around us and our organisation, which is proactively focused on reducing conflict and promoting acceptance. It is not an easy option, but profoundly affects the prosperity of all those concerned. It is non-litigious. It is not 'rights' oriented – however important those rights might be. And it is a choice many people and organisations are deliberately making. (You and yours may be one of them.) Medically, our physical bodies do not like an aggressive ecology. Tests show that the frame of mind we are in directly affects our digestive processes. People are less able to digest food when they are angry or resentful. The system tends to close down. As a doctor once told his patient, 'Its not so much what you eat but what's eating you!' Our bodies are not designed to harbour resentments, attitudes of revenge and other emotionally toxic substances.

Wise people and wise organisations foster a conciliation ecology. The corporate energy is directed to drawing together and harnessing all the strengths within and around the organisation so that it becomes more fruitful, less distracted, more focused, forgiving, honouring and respectful.

Read the true story below:

In 1942 a Signals engineer called Eric Lomax was serving in Singapore when the Allied Forces surrendered to the Japanese. Lomax was marched, with fifty or sixty thousand other men, to the deadly Changi Jail, and transported to Ban Pong to work on the legendary bridge over the river Kwai on the Thai-Burma railway.

Lomax started to secretly make escape equipment, was arrested, and forced to stand outside in the blistering heat all day without food and drink. He was clubbed unconscious and left lying on the ground unattended for days. He had suffered multiple fractures to his nose, both arms, right hip and several ribs due to the violence of the beating. Following further systematic torture, including being caged in a crippling bamboo 'coffin' in the Military Police HQ, he was incarcerated for five years in the infamous Outram Road Jail.

Of all his torturers, a man called Nagase, was particularly horrendous. Lomax decided that he would remember Nagase for the rest of his life, and that one day he would take revenge. Five years later the war ended, he was freed, and was brought back to Britain, suffering violent nightmares, and obsessed by terrifying memories, and other serious psychological traumas.

Still damaged forty-five years later, he read a magazine article in the early 1990's about Nagase, who had written a book about the war. Nagase's book described his remorse at treating the POWs so badly, especially one man, a British prisoner. Lomax recognised himself and wrote to Nagase.

The two men eventually met at the WWII Museum in Kauchaiabui. As Lomax watched Nagase approach, he saw that his tormentor was trembling and in tears. They sat in silence for a time, then Nagase started to say over and over again through his tears, 'I am sorry. I am sorry. Please forgive me for what I did to you.'

The two men spent several days together and got to know each other in a remarkable way. When Lomax eventually left he gave Nagase a note which read:

'Although I can't forget the ill-treatment at Kauchaiabui, taking into account your change of heart, your apologies, and the work you are doing, please accept my total forgiveness.'

1. What punishment do you think would have been fair for Nagase?
2. What compensation would you give to Lomax?
3. Do you think Lomax's final decision was wise? Why?
4. How does this attitude apply to conflicts and injustices in your own life, family or organisation?
5. Think of some examples of both conflict and conciliation. What was the outcome?

30. **A Financial Bonus!**

Here is a pay-off for those in business:

Meet Steve and Jo (real people) who are two senior managers in a 130-strong company – one of our clients. They had a conflict problem. They met once a week and fought for an hour until one of them gave in. It was usually Steve.

Jo confided to our consultant that their meetings should take no more than five minutes, without the self-generated conflict, and that there would also be:

- no personal and departmental 'bruising'
- no productivity loss in the following two hours 'recovery time' and
- a happier atmosphere in both departments for the rest of the day

In a year, their own lost time had cost the company a minimum £3,500. The actual cost of their strife in lost business, surrounding relational damage, avoidance, poor performance, copied behaviour, morale, etc., was huge, with £35,000 per annum – the equivalent of a year's salary – being a conservative estimate.

The company was losing £35,000 a year, for just one hour of conflict a week between only two people and there were dozens of employees behaving like their bosses!

It's worth putting it right.

31. **Owning the Rubbish**

Meet Ian and Cindy . . .

Ian and Cindy live in British Columbia, Canada. They have a lovely family home that is frequently filled with interesting people. Cindy is a counsellor and Ian is a psychiatric nurse. They are a great family! They get a lot of snow which builds up, layer upon layer, throughout the winter and melts eventually in the spring.

Ian and Cindy looked out of their house one day towards the end of winter and saw that the snows of the last few months had melted at last. However the past months had left a load of rubbish all over their front garden. Ian recognised used crisp packets from the kid next door. Cindy reacted to the dog mess deposited in the late evening hours on the dog-walk of the woman five doors down. School children on the way back from school had discarded their sweet wrappers over the fence too. Even the wind had played a part in the mess, with a potato sack blown in from the nearby shop and some branches were down.

Ian and Cindy did not like or want the mess. They wanted it cleared up.

In this story . . .

- Who was responsible for the mess getting into their garden? Mainly other people – and the wind.
- What chance is there that those actually responsible for the mess will clear it up? No chance.
- Ian and Cindy want a clean, tidy front garden. Which of the following two methods do you think will achieve their goal most effectively?
    1. Going to those responsible and demanding they remove their rubbish. (What effect would that have on their neighbourly relationships?)

2. Accepting responsibility for the garden – complete with the mess – and going and clearing it up themselves.
- How can Ian and Cindy stop this happening next winter? They can't. Such is the nature of this world that rubbish does collect in such a fashion!

Here's the challenge!

How do you think this incident applies to our lives, the 'rubbish' we collect and the mess we sometimes find? It doesn't take a rocket scientist to know that you and I unwillingly collect other people's rubbish – their anger, their resentment, their violence, their rejection, their verbal abuse – and a lot of it sticks to us. Some people have gathered so much for so long that they smell terrible. Refusing to clean themselves, other people's rubbish has become rotten and putrid, caked on over many years. Their language has become foul and the maggots of bitterness have eaten away at their self-esteem and personal pride. They blame everyone else for their state, and in a way they are right.

But so what? Is it really worth being right when it leaves us in such a state? If you are that person, wouldn't it be wiser – and such a relief – to remove your stained and ugly clothes and wash away the evidence of the stinking past? It may have been others' fault that you got so soiled, no one is denying that, but you can't blame others that you have stayed that way.

I have seen hundreds of people whose lives have been tarnished by being demeaned and abused by people who knew better. None of us can escape the knocks of life. Most of us get our share.

The answer is to forgive those who hurt us, and keep on forgiving. Sometimes just like Cindy and Ian's garden, the past rubbish blows in again, and we have to collect it up regularly and eject it once more . . . then go and have a bath.

Last year a dad came to me for some coaching. He was around fifty. He had a daughter who had stormed out of their home in her teenage years and been very cold towards him. He hurt inside. I suggested that he forgive her, to which he replied that he thought he had. On the way home from the session in my office he decided to forgive her quite deliberately again.

It was a few weeks later that he had the opportunity to speak to her about it. She was now in her mid twenties, and an adult. The opportunity arose for him to tell her, quite informally, of the struggle he had had, and that he had forgiven her. She burst into tears and hugged him, something she had never ever done before, even as a small child. When he saw me next he told me how wonderful it was to 'have his daughter back'.

Whoever is at fault, forgive them. Bitterness is so destructive, and will destroy your happiness long before it destroys anyone else.

Learning to Forgive

Although forgiving and apologising are very powerful processes that many people have not been taught as children, it is never too late to learn them. They affect relationships very significantly. If you do not either apologise when it is your fault or forgive when it is the other person's fault you will not be able to get properly free of the past and live the future with complete freedom. You may need to practice forgiving a number of times for the same offence.

Instructions:

When you are doing the forgiving, it is certainly not necessary to speak to the person themselves – that can do damage.

Find some privacy, imagine that person standing in front of you and speak 'to them' out loud. Tell them that you forgive them completely and no longer hold them responsible for the repair of the damage in your life. Tell them slowly and deliberately. This can be quite emotional for some people because it releases something deep within us and we tend to release things through tears. That's OK though. A good cry washes all sorts of tensions away.

About Revenge

Revenge is based in a strong sense of personal justice. It assumes you have all the information, know all the motives and facts and are right. Some big assumptions there!

And of course justice is a very powerful motivator. We want to 'get even' with our adversary, and/or punish them. We want to see them suffer somehow. In so doing we make

Objectivity eludes us all

ourselves feel powerful. We tend to carry out our 'just revenge' until we feel better or 'avenged'.

However, revenge is by nature rarely 'just'. Our pain drives us to go far beyond what we would objectively regard as just and fair. We carry on until we feel we have obviously beaten the other person, not just got even. (Beaten is an interesting word in this context!) Never assume you are being objective in avenging yourself or someone you care about. You are compromised and biased.

The most common way we exact revenge is by talking about a person in a damaging way to all and sundry. Forgiveness is a much more powerful response to injustice, and has amazing healing properties for both parties. Forgiving gives you a better sort of power in a relationship. It takes grievances out of circulation and provides a foundation for reconciliation.

32. Apologise Properly

We *forgive* when *others* are wrong. We *apologise* when *we* are wrong. Both forgiving and apologising have amazing power to change the future.

Learning to apologise

The key point about apologising is to do it wholeheartedly. This is much harder for some people than others, but well worth it in the long run. Apologising properly sets both you and the other person free.

Remember to say, 'I am sorry that . . .' rather than 'I'm sorry if . . . .' Get out clauses ('if') stop apologies working properly. Here is another example: 'I'm sorry that you . . . .' Try instead 'I'm sorry that I . . . .' Partial freedom isn't really freedom at all.

Forgiving is done privately, and the forgiveness shown in our behaviour towards the forgiven person. Apologise directly, either in person, or in writing, or by phone if they are further away, for the action to have full effect. Some people think it is humbling, but I think it is very empowering, and it sets both of you free!

Write down the names or initials of people you need to apologise to, then do it and live free.

33. Grow Trust . . . Again?

Can trust re-grow? Just like a tree, trust is an organic, changing thing. New trust can grow where the old trust died. It will definitely be different. Because it is a better-informed trust it can often turn out to be much more reliable.

Trust is like a tree . . .

1. Trust is easily planted. You grow up with your life dependent on others and you will trust them completely.
2. The variety you plant is the variety that will grow.
3. Trust is a living thing and needs room to develop. It is usually fed by seeing what happens to the secrets and snippets of information we share.
4. It is a source of beauty and pleasure – and shelter to others. 'He was so trusting!' We love that kind of vulnerability.
5. It needs tending. It must be fed, protected and respected – particularly in its early stages.
6. It bears fruit like itself – more trust. If you are trustworthy in small things you will be trustworthy in bigger ones. If you are untrustworthy in small things you will be untrustworthy in the bigger ones.
7. It gets more resilient as time goes by. That is what long-term friendship is all about. It is also the reason why broken trust after so many years is so utterly devastating.
8. It will always be vulnerable to some extent. You will never have 100% guarantees when it comes to trust. There is always the faintest possibility of some sort of betrayal . . . 0.02%?
9. If what is above the ground (the branches) outgrows what is below the ground (the roots) it becomes unstable.
10. A damaged or diseased tree can usually be saved if caught and

> Trust is proven in the little everyday things of life

treated soon enough, so too can damaged trust. Don't leave it: get in and sort it out straight away.

11. Initial stages of deterioration are not immediately obvious. Trees often rot from the inside.

12. Even a tree cut down to its roots can eventually grow again. It will grow differently – often stronger and better rooted.

13. It is better for trust to be properly terminated than rot to death. If trust is gone, be honest about that and have a proper conversation about how things are 'right now.' Always leave space for fresh trust to grow – in the next generation?

14. When it is finally gone its fruit can actually last forever.

. . . Anything else?

34. Express Gratitude

Say thank you and mean it.

'Thank you' is so easy to say and does so much. And when you say it, let it come from a heart that lives grateful for small things as well as large ones.

Decide from now on not to let small acts of kindness go unnoticed. It is always possible to find something to say thank you for.

It is always possible to be grateful for something

Perhaps your son cleared up for a change. Instead of 'Its about time too!' try instead, 'Thank you for doing that Paul. I really appreciate it.' It may be appropriate to thank him in front of another person. For men, in particular, a 'public' thank you often provides the recognition they need. To generalise a bit, most men like thanks strong and short, without emotion. Most women like thanks to be a little more emotional and wordy. Whatever happens, keep it sincere.

Men, remember your lady would prefer lots of little sincere thank yous, with perhaps a card or a little gift, rather than one big present every year. (That is your style, not hers!) Women LOVE attention – being noticed and having someone interested in them.

Ladies, men LOVE approval. They will do (almost) anything to keep approval moving in their direction! Genuine 'Thank yous' are a great way to provide that heartfelt approval.

For more on this theme read Dr John Gray's famous book '*Men are from Mars, Women are from Venus*'. It has helped millions of people. I've used so many of his perspectives in my coaching of partnerships, marriages and relationships. They are very practical. To you, John Gray, THANK YOU!

An attitude of gratitude

An attitude of gratitude sharpens your senses to where appreciation and thanks are needed. This week I went out and thanked the men who empty our dustbins. I guess not many people say thank you to them, but am I grateful! There was no patronage on my part, no hidden motive.

Sometimes a proper thank you is worth far more than the tip that may go with it. After all, life consists not of the abundance of possessions. It consists of connections between people. Relationships are fed with words. Good words build, nurture and restore. Careless, harmful words are like bad food that is spilt on the floor and lies rotting in the dark corners of relationships. It feeds the disease-infested rats, the serpents and cockroaches of life that eventually poison us and bite our children when we are off our guard.

Express gratitude. Say thank you often.

35. The Paradox of Tough Times

Let me guess: you have been through some tough times recently?

You are not alone. Many men and women, and sadly many children and young people too, live their whole lives facing and handling tough times.

Our family has not had it that tough, although for a year, not so long ago, we were on 'Family Credit,' the British government safety net for those below the poverty line. (It is a very low poverty line!) As a family we have experienced the emotionally debilitating trauma of betrayal and significant rejection – from people we profoundly trusted and still love. I have come very close to a nervous breakdown, in the past, through stress and overwork.

Our eldest daughter contracted a serious, incurable disease when she was 19 years old. We are a very close family, and I can't begin to tell you what her illness did to my wife and me.

Failing is success trying to be born

We have experienced the deep down feelings of panic that come to those who face circumstances beyond their control. We have found ourselves forced to think differently, act differently and live differently.

We have walked with close friends, clients and colleagues through the deep agony of their bankruptcy, cruel injustice, divorce, physical assault and bereavement. My wife was only 28 when she lost her mum through cancer. Her mum was 52.

You're only a 'failure' if you actually quit

But we have not experienced what you've been through. Only you have done that. Your tough times may have been, or may be still, a lot more painful than ours. You may want to run away, or quit, or commit suicide, or divorce, or resign, or whatever.

Someone to blame

It is very tempting in tough times to look for a scapegoat, someone to blame. We want to know who put us where we are, and then we fantasise about what we will do to them. We'll make them sorry, hurt them back, make them apologise, take them to court, get even, force them to make amends, or grovel, or take responsibility for what they did to us and those we love. We want to ruin their reputation, warn everyone else of what they're like and, if we could seriously get away with it, even kill them.

Like you, I've felt most of those reactions – particularly over pain that my family has experienced and has certainly not deserved. Choosing for these things to make me better, not bitter, has been very challenging. How will I deal with tough times, especially when I know I didn't 'deserve' them?

As you know, this book is not designed as a 'smile and forget it' palliative, gimmicky and shallow to make you feel better short-term. Your future happiness depends on how you choose to react when things go badly, when they don't work out the way you think they should have done, or the way you believed you deserved – and you probably did! Circumstances and market forces do not bow to our personal preferences or gently respond to our needs. It is us who must adapt, develop and adjust.

Tough times never last, but tough people do. The toughest people are those who do not compromise their values and principles, yet are ready to bend their wills and lives to adjust to some of the stronger forces at work in our world.

Tough isn't brittle. Tough does not mean 'hard as nails'. Tough does not mean insensitive – though it probably does mean sensitive in the right places and a little less sensitive in the others!

Tough means being patient and kind. It means refusing to envy, boast or be proud. Being tough does not mean being rude or self-seeking. It means not being easily angered and keeping no record of wrongs. Scapegoats are not on the menu. Tough people do not delight in evil but go for the truth every time and are pleased when it triumphs. When you're tough you protect people, risk trusting them, maintain hope, persevere.

Tough means sticking with the vision, taking a lead, and moving things forward. It can also mean stepping back from the plan for a time, allowing another person to take the lead, putting things on hold, accepting that this idea is not going to work.

We all admire the best sorts of toughness, yet both emotional and mental toughness, like human muscle, is only developed by working against the resistances of life – swimming upstream when it is easier to go with the flow.

Only dead fish float down the river

Toughness may also involve a reduction in the popularity stakes. You will often be on your own. I'm not entirely sure which is the chicken and which is the egg, but toughness and aloneness go together pretty regularly.

Most people drift through life, taking the easier option. I think it was Walt Whitman who wrote

> *'Two paths met in a wood, and I,*
> *I took the path less travelled by.'*

If you want a better life, to outrun the rat race, to enrich your life, then don't be seduced by the easier choices, go for the tougher ones, the ones that will truly develop you, challenge you, strengthen you, and empower you. Don't try to buy your way out. Allow them to have their effect – co-operate with them. You will emerge a better person.

36. Choose to Lead

'I'm not a Leader'

Do you just follow the crowd most of the time? Or let other people dictate what you do, how you spend your money, and what you think? Do your children make you live in a particular way? Are you in charge of them, or are they in charge of you? You'll know by now that doesn't help you or them. Neither young children, nor teenagers are designed or equipped to be head of your household – you are!

Secondary Leadership

Let's look at leading others. Secondary Leadership is about becoming aware of the influence you have and, quite deliberately, choosing how you are going to do that. You can use your skills and abilities to influence other people for good and make this world a better place to live in.

All of us have those abilities. For some they are underdeveloped and weak. Some people regard influencing others as somehow wrong, dangerous, or to be avoided for other reasons.

Tolerance of others is often a good quality, but you should not tolerate being led or influenced in a direction that you know is not helpful or good.

37. Influence Before Prominence

I was asked recently to write a short motivating article for a business paper, and following its publication I received a phone call from a businessman I didn't know. He explained that he owned a garage, had been in quite some personal turmoil and was on the point of giving up, quitting his car repair business for good. He told me that as he read what I had written, he knew he had to press through, saying how important the article had been to him in making his decision. His phone call was a real encouragement to me too.

I want to be as influential as I can be, without being particularly prominent. Prominence may come, but as any public figure will tell you, it is a mixed blessing. Some of the most influential people in our culture are unknown, hidden from public view. They are quietly working to better society with their medical research, business skills or political activity. Recognition is not high on their list of motivating factors. They just want their life here on this planet to have made a difference.

One list of influential people that can never be published is the list of mothers and fathers who have lovingly believed in their children and encouraged them to fulfil their potential, to make a difference. If you are a parent or grandparent, give your children or grandchildren that essential personal confidence and self-esteem necessary to walk past the negative influences of life and achieve their goals.

Another list will be of school teachers. I am amazed at the dedication and sheer effort that goes into being a good teacher. A class teacher of thirty or so eight-year-olds will have invested an entire year of his/her life with each of 1,100 individual children during a career span of thirty-five years. That's influence! If each of those children were to go on and do the same good because of that teacher, they would influence over 1.2 million people in just one generation!

The knock-on effect of influence is very motivating. Who are you influencing? We all influence somewhere. It is impossible not to. Perhaps you are a captain of industry, with a board of eager directors or young managers who copy your style and imitate your attitude. Perhaps you are one of those managers.

Whoever you are, remember that, although prominence may sometimes be important, influence comes before prominence in the list of priorities.

38. Influence by Example

'Example is not the best way to influence people; it's the only way.'

Albert Schweitzer.

Irrespective of what you say, people will follow what you do. From the moment you were born you have learnt by observing the behaviour of those around you and doing what they do. You imitate them. And you are well practised and competent at it.

Those closest to you, or those who spend most time around you will imitate you – especially if you are important to them as a perceived role model.

The manager who declares 'Don't do what I do, do what I say', will eventually be copied by all those who report to him. They in turn will learn to live out his example and henceforth declare 'Don't do what I do, do what I say!'

As my family were growing up, we had a meal together each evening. When the children were growing up we wanted them to gain some acceptable table manners, which for us excluded elbows on the table. They had to be reminded of this from time to time. Eventually it came out, 'But Daddy, you've got your elbows on the table!'

I gave the children permission to politely point out this little habit when I unwittingly transgressed. From then on, of course, we all had to watch out!

What have I taught those around me? What am I teaching them now?

I am presently coaching a client, whose parents gave him a terrible example of how to behave – rows, violence, neglect, rejection, selfishness – and a whole lot more. He said to me recently that he was looking to me to coach him in learning new ways of behaving as an adult, and would follow my mentoring. He was looking for another model, one that he could respect and be proud to imitate.

Our family was out in the countryside one day when I asked one of the children what they thought God was like. It was a shock as well as a challenge when the ten-year-old replied 'A bit like you Daddy really.' It was a profound reminder of how important my example was. I must also confess here that I've got a little way to go yet in that particular modelling scenario!

I was visiting a company recently in my work as a consultant, and was fascinated yet again by how the Managing Director's style had been copied by his younger directors. Mike was a very influential MD. His office was part of the boardroom. He had a high back chair, a big black desk prominently across one end of the board-table, lots of chrome, glass and dark wood, and his 21-inch computer monitor dominating proceedings – just his style! Interestingly each of his directors own offices had a scaled down version of almost the same, the layout, the colours, the power, even though they were quite different people when I got to know them better. These were very bright individuals, not copycats. Their behaviour indicates again the power of a role model and they were surprised by just how much when we pointed it out!

The Japanese vacuum-cleaner salesman

'Yet me show you!'

There is an apocryphal story about a passionate Japanese vacuum-cleaner salesman who could only say the words 'Yet me show you!' He arrived on housewives' doorsteps with his demonstration vacuum cleaner held high, smiling broadly and declaring 'Yet me show you!'

'Can it do curtains?'

'Yet me show you!'

'Upholstery?'

'Yet me show you!'

He sold millions.

39. Aim for INTER-Dependence

In just about every context, we can do more together than we can working in isolation; the whole is greater than the sum of its parts; or . . .

1+1=3, 4, 5, etc.

We were physically created using that process – by two independent people co-operating closely together to produce a new baby. It is a law of nature, seen throughout the universe. Even in conflict, when two forces collide in an apparently destructive way new things emerge.

The odd and interesting thing about the following three stages is that they do not have strongly defined cut-off points. We can still be dependent in one area of life, and largely independent in another. Inter-dependence is always the goal though, if we are to enjoy the richness of a better life.

In the living world of animals and plants the process can usually be simplified into these three stages. The new baby will experience . . .

Stage 1. Dependence

A perfectly normal state for smaller children, those experiencing times of ill health, old age, etc. The newly created person needs to learn madly, grow in strength, discover and refine new skills, absorbing the nourishment it needs for Stage 2.

Emotionally, intellectually and spiritually, you are initially dependent on others to guide, inspire, feed and protect you. This 'First Age' of life is one of needing others for your very existence.

Some people never get beyond Dependence. They remain subtly (sometimes blatantly) dependent on others, looking to them for their daily needs and keeping others under the impression that it is the others' duty to supply what is needed, and their own right to have it.

Human beings devise all sorts of neat little systems and tricks to stay dependent on other people and save themselves the trauma and personal cost of accepting personal responsibility.

Leaving home and making our own way can be a bit risky, so we can't have that! However we all know the sadness that accompanies people who never grow up, who stay as children, and we recognise it as a disability. This can be physical, emotional or intellectual immaturity.

Stage 2. Independence

For most of us there is a lot of pleasure in Stage 2. Stage 2 is usually a choice. Without it we will never move to the wholesomeness of Inter-dependence. Without the inner freedom essential to independence, inter-dependence, Stage 3, is impossible. Unless we are independent we are not free to choose to commit. Instead we will bring all the other people, on whom we are still dependent, with us.

Dave brought his mother into his relationship with his partner. She isn't physically there, of course . . . well, come to think of it, she might be! But she is there manipulating in the background, actively influencing, subtly, perhaps quite subconsciously, making things happen her way – through Dave.

Sharon is dependent on an old boyfriend, Ryan, who eventually left her six months ago. She never really got free of him, and her new partner lives with the collective memories of Ryan as a ghostly standard to live up to and be like. Sharon needs to leave Ryan behind and become independent again. Only then is she ready for an inter-dependent relationship.

This Second Age of life, where we have largely broken free of the security lines of childhood and adolescence, has its own particular joys. We can look forward, 'hassle-free', to decisions about who we are going to co-operate with in life: An employer? A life-partner? Who knows!

Independence is easily eroded. Employers, partners, family, have a vested interest in having people dependent on them. Dependent people are easily controlled – and exploited. Independent ones are not.

Independence is about coming to maturity, taking calculated risks and accepting responsibility for the consequences of the decision. More mistakes are made here and lessons learnt, but it's an essential step.

Stage 3. Inter-dependence

Independent people exercising the choice of working together with others for the common good.

This is the goal: a lifetime of free, fruitful and rewarding inter-dependence!

Inter-dependent relationships can be long-term (I've had the same doctor for fifteen years) or short term (I filled up my car at a different service station yesterday) and anything in between. The delight of such relationships is their flexibility and usefulness. I do not need to know all about how my body works because David my doctor does. I have no need to carry cans of fuel – I can buy it from someone else miles away. Any commitment is a chosen one, to our mutual benefit, and can be quite narrowly defined. It is based on trust, and inevitably demands an act of faith.

40. **Stop Touching Wood**

'I haven't had a car accident yet, touch wood.'

In psychology 'touching wood' is known as a sort of anchor, something we do to bring a particular feeling to ourselves. For instance, the smell of farmyard manure takes me straight back to my childhood days (I was brought up on a dairy farm), and talk of skiing makes me want to put my feet together and bend my knees! So 'touching wood' makes us feel that we are not 'tempting Fate' after all, relieves our fears and makes us feel that the future is now that much safer.

Revealed fear?

However, the fear of the unknown, revealed by 'touching wood', is a fear we can do without – a fear of some potentially harmful power that has influence over our life and which needs to be appeased or pacified by a superstitious action – touching wood.

Why give thought-space to such an influence – whether real or imagined? Such fears can be powerful and do not serve us well. Your life will not be undermined when you talk positively about the things you hope for in the future or talk gratefully about the past. Nor will you be saved from disappointment by touching wood or any other similar practice. Disappointment is here to stay, along with all the other feelings we experience!

41. **Prepare Yourself**

I was sitting in a boring meeting early in 1996. The speaker was droning on for his allotted half hour or so when into my mind came a line written in a letter centuries ago to a young Greek called Timothy: 'Prepare your mind for action.' I had no work and didn't know what to do. I was, as the Americans say 'between a rock and a hard place.'

The temptation to surrender to 'Fate' at these moments is huge. 'Give up, see what happens, what will be will be.' Absolutely not! All around are vast opportunities to serve, to gain, to learn – if only I could see them and access them. There would be ways in to the opportunities of life and I would need to find them. I knew that readiness to change is, invariably, the key and that the proof of learning is altered behaviour. To 'prepare my mind for action' meant removing anything that would limit my ability to learn, adapt and respond, and grabbing hold of everything relevant and available to read, mark, learn and inwardly digest. It meant disconnecting myself from the unhealthy perception that my future may be governed by star signs, crystals, tarot cards or a fortune-teller's imagination.

What are you actually doing when you surrender your cause to 'Fate'?

You are opting out of proper preparation. As a businessman once said, 'When I work hard I get lucky, when I don't I don't.' The formula I use is:

'Luck' = Preparation + Opportunity

The secret, if there is one, is to:

1. Put in lots of preparation
2. Create and recognise opportunities.

If you keep your senses alert you will see all sorts of opportunities that are there for the taking – and you can take them IF you are as prepared as you can be. There is no 'get-out' clause here. No one is 'unlucky' in exams. They just didn't work hard enough to get a good grade at the right subject areas. The purpose of preparation is to enable us to recognise and take the opportunities that come. You never know what opportunities you will get this week. You can prepare for them though.

Practice making changes

Keep both your physical and mental faculties flexible and in good health, so that when opportunities arise you can take advantage of them quickly. Embrace change; see it as a friend that will bring new and fresh resources to you.

Expect them

That is reasonable, for opportunities arrive for everyone – we just don't quite know when.

'We will never surrender!' – Sir Winston Churchill

In your preparation, focus on what is inside, on 'skeleton,' not 'scaffolding'. Scaffolding is ugly, rigid, external, and temporary.

Your skeleton is hidden neatly away, part of you, and amazingly flexible. It supports your whole body from within and enables you to eat your sandwich and travel the world!

Take your pick.

Occasionally your skeleton goes wrong and demands attention. It may break and need a temporary 'bone' on the outside whilst it heals. Happily, most of the time, for most of us, it is brilliant.

What are your core beliefs, your skeleton? How do they affect your attitudes?

Here is an example of a core belief about people. One of these will apply to you. The other three won't:

1. Everyone is basically bad.

2. Everyone is basically good.
3. Some of us are basically bad whilst others of us are basically good.
4. Within each of us is both good and bad. We are all both good and bad.

Whatever good or bad may mean, one of those principles will govern the relationship you have with everyone you know and most of the people you don't:

'Joseph didn't mean to beat up Martin.' Which belief is reflected here?

How about: 'I never trust a stranger'?

Your core belief system will also affect the attitude you have towards yourself – 'I am basically a good (bad, or whatever) person.'

My choice is number 4. What are those core beliefs again?

Live beyond merely taking on other people's beliefs and values and bolting them together like scaffolding around weak architecture. Prepare yourself, your mind, for action. Establish properly inter-linked, alive and functioning principles for the core of your life that provide form and strength for the outer life you live. And don't misuse them.

42. **Cave Walking**

Imagine yourself half way into a long, narrow cave: the sun is shining outside.

When you are afraid or insecure, do you tend to run and hide yourself at the back of the cave, or come out into the light?

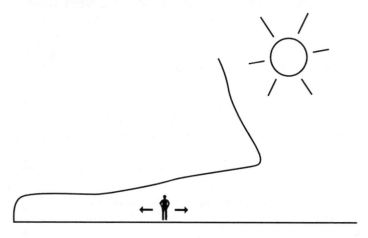

The back of the cave seems the safest place to be and the temptation is to put your head under the blankets, to use a different metaphor, and hope it all goes away.

This is never truer than when it comes to debt. Debt and creditors (the people to whom you owe money) do not easily go away. And debt has an unnerving tendency to get much bigger with time. Hiding NEVER works, and plays havoc with your self worth. Facing the truth, about how much you are in debt and to whom, is essential before a way out of debt is to be found.

> Hiding
> never
> works.
> You are
> safer in
> the light

Gordon's reaction to the realities of life – especially the bank statement – was highly predictable.

The back of the cave provides a very false sense of security. Walk out of the cave by asking yourself:

- Is there anything in my life I am refusing to face?
- Am I hiding from anything?
- Am I being slightly dishonest with myself at all?
- About what?
- What would I find if I brought everything out into the light?

Make sure you are crystal clear on this:

1. Start by admitting that there are things!
2. Then note down what those things actually are.
3. Be honest with a close friend about it all.
4. Plan a course of action.
5. Do it.

It is so releasing to be walking in the light instead of the murky grey shadows of cave dwellers.

By the way, there are a number of very good debt counselling charities around. If that is your problem, use one.

43. Try 'No Reason' Generosity

'Here is a simple rule of thumb for behaviour: ask yourself what you want people to do for you; then grab the initiative and do it for them – free! If you only love the loveable, what do you expect? A pat on the back? If you only give for what you hope to get out of it, don't pretend that's charity. The stingiest pawnbrokers do that . . .

Give away your life; you'll find life given back, but not merely given back – given back with bonus and blessing. Giving, not getting, is the way forward.'

The Message

Generous means giving more than is due

An attitude of generosity affects a person's outlook on life in general and is well worth the apparent loss. See giving as an investment in future generations. One benefit for us is that it deals with the meanness that so easily creeps in.

I was sitting recently with a group of teachers who did the National Lottery as a consortium every week. We were discussing what they would do if they won it. I was amazed, and disappointed too, to hear one of them say that the two million pounds each would receive wouldn't be enough to give any away. 'Well, you can spend that much can't you!'

What would be the basis for your decision?

If we only give money away when we can't manage to spend it ourselves what sort of example is that?

Meanness cripples the spirit, devalues the needy and is a lousy model for the next generation to follow.

Perhaps you have already decided to be generous for no reason, to give some of what you have to another person, simply because you have it and they don't. Who was it said, when asked why he climbed Everest, that he did it 'because it's there'? What a brilliant reason for being generous – 'because the money is there –

and so are those in need.'

Here are a couple of ideas for you to try:

- Buy a book you've been really looking forward to reading, and give it to a friend – without reading it!
- Decide not to watch your favourite TV programme and devote your attention to someone else during that time.

How 'sad' is this quote!

'I can't give because, by the time I have paid my bills, handled the credit card debt, sorted out my subscription to the sports club, paid off the car, the pension fund standing order, gone on holiday, put some savings aside, and drawn out enough cash to live on, I don't have disposable income to give away.'

Mother Theresa of Calcutta said *'The more we have, the less we can give.'*

Why do you think she said that?

44. Knowing or Enquiry?

Jim McNeish is another canny Scot. He is in his thirties and very clever. He is Head of Learning and Development in a very influential international company. Oh, and he is very honest in a loving sort of way.

One warm summer's evening, Jim was over with our family for a barbecue. We love having him and he feels at home with us. The three children were all home from University, etc., and we had a great time, chatting avidly about all the bigger issues of life. Jim's stimulating contributions from his psychology and philosophy background, his leading questions and gentle prodding are excellent 'grist to the mill'. He is great, and always reminds me of how much we can encourage people by endorsing and honouring them. Jim does that all the time.

Later, after our discussions, just as he was getting into his car to go home, Jim asked me a life-changing question – and I want to ask it of you today.

The conversation went like this:

Jim: *'Andrew, what would it take for you to move from a position of knowing to a position of enquiry?'*
Me: *'I am in a position of enquiry.'*
Jim: *'That's a position of knowing.'*
(Long pause from me)
Me: *'Help me.'*
Jim: *'That is a position of enquiry.'*

I learned a great deal in those few seconds. That question changed me. I had been justifying myself, that evening, over a particular decision I had made and was ignoring others' views. A knowing position. It was distorting my views and preventing me from learning anything new or gaining anything fresh. I asked Jim for help, at that moment, because I respect him and trust him. By asking for help I broke the lock on the door of that part of my thinking allowing a much more inquisitive and helpful approach.

None of us has all the answers. Like a gigantic jigsaw puzzle life unfolds with each of us contributing our part. However, we badly need each other's particular piece to see the complete picture.

The New Testament says *'Ask and it shall be given you. Seek and you shall find. Knock and the door will be opened.'* All of these three involve us deliberately setting out on a path of discovery.

What would it take for you to move from a position of knowing to a position of enquiry?

45. Have the Courage of Your Convictions

Consider Cassie Burnall

Cassie was in the library at Colombine High School in Denver, Colorado and hid behind her desk as the two Trenchcoat Mafiosi, Eric Harris and Dylan Klebold, burst in brandishing guns. One of the killers put a semi-automatic pistol to the side of her head and asked: 'Do you believe in God?' Cassie looked back at him and answered 'Yes'. He pulled the trigger.

No one doubts that Cassie died asserting her faith and probably for it. Either way, as someone in the town put it, 'Why did they ask her? Because they knew what she was.' Maybe the psychopath killer would have destroyed Cassie whatever she had said to him, but one thing is unquestionable – she would not deny her faith when faced with a violent death.

The response to Cassie's courage is staggering. 73,000 teenagers attended a rally in honour of her. All the major newspapers in America wrote about her. The '*Weekly Standard*' devoted twelve pages to Cassie's story. The '*Chicago Tribune*' wrote of Cassie Burnall 'She could have lied – but she didn't. She could have fudged or quibbled – but she didn't. She simply said 'Yes.'

What would you die for?

46. **Hero Worship**

We all worship something or someone – Hindus search for Brahman, Buddhists for enlightenment. Islam declares 'There is no God but God, and Muhammad is the prophet of God.' We may worship our families, ourselves, our possessions or our animals.

Like 1,700 million other people on this planet (according to Encyclopaedia Britannica) I live in a culture formed predominantly out of the Christian tradition. I have chosen, and am personally committed to those Christian roots, and my hero is Jesus Christ.

The more I study Christ's teaching, the more convinced I am that I want to follow him. It is truly revolutionary! If everyone decided to adhere to this life-transforming stuff the world really would be a different place.

Take a look:

- There would be no children suffering the agony of divorce.
- No unfaithfulness, no affairs. No rejection.
- There would be no burglar alarms going off at night. No theft, no locks on the doors. No car thieves.
- The legal profession would be redundant. No litigation, no courts, no need for police, no fear.
- Our children would be safe in the street and in the park. No abduction, no pornography, no drug abuse.
- We would all care for each other. No starving people, no revenge, no wars.
- Everyone would be trustworthy and trusting.
- There would be hope, joy, acceptance, honouring, reward, laughter, safety, fun . . .

That is why I worship Jesus Christ and promote his teaching. He offers not just 'pie in the sky when you die' as a wit once described Heaven, but 'steak on a plate while you wait'.

(Apologies to all vegetarians!)

Heaven on earth – what a way to live!

A footnote to this chapter

I was discussing this chapter with Campbell recently and he commented that life is a one-way ticket with a destination. He suggested I remind you that you do not need to walk the road alone and that God has a gift for you. He freely and generously provides his supernatural wisdom and guidance to all those who ask him.

Good, eh?

(Campbell is such a special person – I so wish you could meet him!)

47. **Practise Saying a Positive 'No'**

Two areas to look at here:

1. *Saying 'No' to other people*
2. *Saying 'No' to yourself*

Both of these have great power to enrich you. Although both can be a challenge, some people struggle most with the first, others with the second!

Know when to say 'No'

People can treat our lives like a rubbish tip, putting their disappointments, guilt and frustration on to us. Usually they are quite unaware of it, although with only a little insight we can identify what is happening! They can also expect you to take actions that violate you and your thinking.

A couple of examples:

- 'My dad was desperate for me to be a doctor. You see, he never went to university.' I will never forget the silence that followed my answer to this fourth-year student's confession that he had never wanted to be a doctor. I suggested he did something else. The thought had never occurred to him.
- 'Everyone fiddles their expenses so I have to or I will embarrass the others.' This 22-year-old was violating her conscience every month. She decided to say 'No' and live free.

Both these people were being manipulated. They had surrendered the freedom to be themselves and go with what they knew was right.

119

Saying 'No' to yourself

Self-control, self-discipline and inner strength go together.

It is not difficult to become grossly overweight, hooked on pornography, or drive too fast when you have lost, or never had, self discipline. We are not talking masochistic austerity here, just plain old self control.

Along with self-control comes inner strength. Denying yourself a luxury item when you simply don't need it, choosing not to eat for a few days (fasting), or giving away some money (generosity) makes you amazingly richer! Your self-esteem goes up, any selfishness is controlled, you become mentally as well as physically fitter. There are so many positives!

Another spin off from this sort of self-control is that you will realise just how much you are subtly pushed around by the advertising industry! Sit down one evening and see how many of the adverts on the television are really honest and truthful.

Credit Cards

My credit card company invited me to buy whatever I wanted. They were prepared to give me even more 'credit' to do so – well, not quite give! I would be paying it back for years, and they would benefit to the tune of 29.5% per annum. Unsurprisingly, self-control prevailed!

Being able to refrain

Being in control of your life, being able to refrain, to say 'No,' brings a wonderful sense of personal power although for the first few times it is a bit of a culture shock. The more we exercise the muscles of self-control, the stronger they get. It costs little more than a dose of determination to stay in control.

Say 'No' sometimes. No one seriously wants a world of greedy hedonistic people – do they?

48. Baker's Dozen on Stress

Thirteen simple de-stressers

1. Simplify
2. Smile and laugh a lot
3. Eat and drink healthily
4. Fill your mind with good, beautiful, positive things (How cute! The thing is, it works!)
5. Work hard and play hard within an organised framework
6. Rest properly
7. Count your blessings every day, and be thankful
8. Find a life target and set realistic personal goals to hit it
9. Forgive and keep your conscience clear – unforgiving people destroy themselves first
10. Exercise vigorously three times a week until you're smiling again (as long as that is OK with your doctor!)
11. Be kind to people – especially those who are not so attractive – and don't expect anything in return
12. Say nice things about yourself (when you are on your own!) and about others when you are with them
13. Dream positively about your future. Hopelessness really is a life-threatening disease

49. **Decide Where You are Going**

Mission statements have got bad press, but the answer to misuse is not non-use. Used properly and with integrity a mission statement can be brilliantly helpful. Used badly or to manipulate, it is worse than useless, a thorough distraction.

For several years now a personal mission statement has focused my life. I have always lived with a fairly clear sense of direction, but putting it into a more formal statement has really helped me gain clarity and control of my life.

A mission statement is a living thing. It is not unchangeable – I adjust mine from time to time – but it is written out for me to see and live by.

One of the best things is actually sitting down and writing it, putting verbal expression to the deepest motives, desires and thoughts. It will enable you to coach yourself and identifies what is really important to you. A mission statement is initially a very private thing, and can be challenging. It may be a little embarrassing as you find it exposing motives and desires that you know are unhelpful to yourself or others. Some people find such a document painful to write because they discover they have no sense of purpose, are going nowhere and have been drifting aimlessly for many a year.

A mission statement promotes personal responsibility. Am I accepting responsibility for who I am, the way I live and what I do? Have I surrendered the leadership of my life to someone else? Am I taking responsibility for my thought life and attitudes as well as my outward behaviour? Am I disciplined in the way I live? We've looked at these elsewhere.

A mission statement develops character. It promotes the growth of endurance, determination, patience, hope, self-control, care for others, etc.

A mission statement actually helps achieve those goals! Our unconscious minds draw us towards them even when we are not

122

consciously 'going for it'. Decisions we make will be affected. We will be less enthusiastic about goals outside our mission statement and more enthusiastic about actions that support it.

One reason for this is that our mission statement reflects who we are. Like an address label on a package, it describes where we are going, our expected destination and often line by line! An unaddressed or inadequately addressed package may eventually end up where intended, but it is more likely to go astray.

Give serious thought to writing a personal mission statement. Take time, perhaps a few weeks, to formulate it in your mind and set aside the best part of a weekend to actually write it. There's no rush.

My Personal Mission Statement

As we get to the end of this book and know each other a bit better I thought you might like to know what my personal Mission Statement is so I've included it. Remember it is personal to me and will change a little as I go along in life. My mission is:

To worship Almighty God alone as Creator, Redeemer, Sustainer of the Universe, and King of all.

To live in the confidence that God has a unique purpose for my life, and for the life of every human being, that reflects his love for me and for mankind.

To work with Him towards the fulfilment of that purpose, guided and empowered by the Holy Spirit, cushioned by God's grace, and accountable to Him.

To cherish the vision of a kind and forgiving world for future generations.

To seek the truth and keep eternity in view.

To teach life-transforming principles with enthusiasm, and to narrow the gap between principle and practice.

(It is amazing how just a few thought-out paragraphs can change your life.)

50. Finish Well

Getting Closure

Whether it is leaving school (wherever you're going next), a resignation (for whatever reason), retirement (at whatever age), a death (however it happened), divorce (whoever's fault) do your best to finish well.

In my years of coaching and counselling I have watched so many people suffer simply because there was no proper 'closure' – no clean straightforward exit from the relationship or circumstance. A messy ending can take so long to clear up in our minds.

Turn the page cleanly

Our logical minds like to have things neat and settled. As a society we have Inquiries and Courts to determine what happened and who was to blame. We like to know. But finishing well is not about fault, or detail. It is about being able to close the door satisfactorily on one stage of life and walk through the next. It is about turning the page with confidence, leaving the past chapter safely behind. It is about turning to the future and letting the past simply stand as it is or was. Not always easy – particularly if it was painful. Who killed her? What did I do wrong? Why doesn't she love me any more? How did I end up here? Why me?

Goodbye with Grace

Do everything you can to make sure that when things end, they end tidily. Many endings are sad but we can close them with grace. Even things like divorce and death can end with dignity and honour, each person looking back on the better times (and there are always some of those if we choose to look for them) with gratitude and expressed appreciation.

Whether you are leaving school, graduating from University, or even being made redundant – even sacked – say thank you for what you have learnt, gained, and benefited from. Employment is a contract to exchange time and energy for cash. When it comes to an end, we can say thank you for the months or years of benefit gained.

'Thank you for having me'

When the children were small they often went to their friends' parties or on little outings. We taught them to say thank you. As we get older we can sometimes forget old courtesies. In our fight for our rights we see it as another's duty towards us to do this or that. A sincerely spoken 'Thank you' can mend so much, and provide a less fraught ending to a painful departure.

And while we are on the subject, I'd like to say 'Thank you' to you for giving me the privilege of addressing you and your life.

Thank you. I've really appreciated it. Go and enjoy the future.

51. **Essential Inner Power**

At the beginning of this book I made it clear that I haven't 'arrived' yet. I'm on the same journey as you, a one-way trip through life to a distant destination. I became particularly aware of the importance of both the journey and the destination as a teenager, and that sense of importance has only grown.

Back then, I was introduced to, and chose to travel the road with, a God-given guide, the Holy Spirit. I innocently invited him to become my 'inner companion' on the adventure and willingly surrendered myself to his influence. It was the best decision I ever made and has proved to be the most life-transforming one.

On the final page of his brilliant book '*Seven Habits of Highly Effective People*' Stephen Covey makes the point that 'as human beings we cannot perfect ourselves'. That is my experience and I'm sure it's yours too. Through thick and thin, through tough times and easy times, God has given me unconditional acceptance, reassurance and strength – and continues to do so. He has become not so much a crutch as a life-support system, a personal coach to help me make the best of each day and each mile. The Holy Spirit is my 'secret weapon' when dealing with the challenges I have to overcome, my essential power-source for living what I've found to be a much better life.